Dear Susan. – I thought you might
be interested in M.R's books.

C

 size does matter

Thank you to my wonderful husband, James, and my gorgeous children, Ben and Madz, for their encouragement, love and support.

size

does

matter

How to Eat, Drink and Lose Weight … Forever

matter

Contents

Many of my years have been in the world of nutrition and dietetics. I have attended conferences, researched, read and written articles, but most of my time has been spent working one to one with clients, guiding them towards their goals. I've listened to thousands of histories of weight loss and weight gain, stories told by people confused, despairing and disappointed in the dense jungle of diet promises.

Introduction

So often, the 'diet' simply hasn't worked, and you don't have to look far to see what is happening as a result. Despite the best intentions of international research and weight loss campaigns at all levels – from individuals taking responsibility themselves through to policy-backed government-funded initiatives – worldwide body weight is tracking steadily upwards.

Throughout my career I've followed recommended guidelines set up by various professional taskforces to target the obesity epidemic. Over the years I've observed how these generalised recommendations certainly haven't delivered results in terms of turning these weight gain trends around. Why is this? It's a question I often go back to. I've spent many hours reviewing different lifestyles and pondering why some clients are so hungry, others lose weight quite easily, while another group struggles on

a daily basis. Right from the beginning I received strong messages from my clients that weight loss wasn't easy, simple or straightforward. In discussions with other health care providers the words 'lazy' and 'unmotivated' have often come up. I am sure this is not the case and, in fact, feel confident that other significant factors have been overlooked.

Size Does Matter involves two aspects of my work as a health professional in the weight loss industry. The first concerns how to find the truth about foods for weight loss as many of the nutrition messages are misunderstood, misleading and often distorted.

The second aspect is about some remarkable technology that totally transformed my practice and my approach to weight loss. The technology shows the amount of muscle mass and body fat in

any one person's body and this information on how an individual's body is made up is, I believe, essential to move ahead with weight loss. This technology has certainly changed the lives of many of my clients. For too long weight loss has been fixated on what to eat and how much exercise to do, and in the process we have totally overlooked the body composition of the individual.

This is not a nutrition book, nor is it a science book. *Size Does Matter* is purely a weight loss book. The first seven chapters will give you important background knowledge about your foods, fluids and exercise. Chapters 8 – 12 will show you how to put this information into action according to your body makeup, in a way that's sustainable without dominating your life. The last chapter is to inspire and encourage you with vegetables, and contains recipes that are quick, easy and tasty.

I believe by reading this book you'll soon be more than ready to put the old soul-destroying diets behind you and move into a positive, enjoyable way of life where success is achieved through knowing the right-size portion for your size.

MaryRose Spence BHSc
NZ Registered Dietitian

> This is not a nutrition book, nor is it a science book. *Size Does Matter* is purely a weight loss book.

It's all about YOU

Focus on you
Cut the ties
Find simple solutions
Fuel yourself

Focus on you

There has never been a diet that has 'worked' and there never will be. While you look for successful weight loss by counting kilojoules or selecting foods that are good or bad, healthy or not healthy, low fat, high fibre, low carbohydrate, high protein and so on, you will never find a solution to your weight problems. That's because a diet designed for *every* body is not designed for *your* body. To succeed at losing weight, you need to understand YOU, before you focus on food. You need to know who you are feeding and what your body makeup is. Only then will you be able to successfully match your food to your requirements.

Consider a group of people, all with the same age, same height and same weight. If they were to eat the same amount and exercise the same amount over a period of time, some would lose weight, some would maintain weight and some would gain weight. There would also be noticeable differences in their appetite. Some would feel hungry within a couple of hours of a meal and need to snack; others would eat and feel satisfied until the next meal was put on the table. Everybody in the group might have the same weight, but each person's body composition would be unique – and that's why each person would have unique food needs.

It's time to take a closer look at your body's composition and find out how different ratios of fat and muscle need to be fed in different ways.

When we were hunters and gatherers, we had to be active over a large part of the day to find our food, and quantities were often not plentiful. This active lifestyle gave us bodies that were all quite similar in composition – high in muscle and low in fat. As it happened, the food that was available to us suited this body makeup.

But over the years, our lives and therefore our food needs, have changed significantly. Many of us now spend our days sitting at a desk. This sedentary lifestyle, together with the development of cars, remote controls, machines and computers – technology designed to save us time and energy – means it has become easy to be inactive. 'Hunting and gathering' is now simply a matter of pushing a trolley around a supermarket and popping items into it. We live in a country where there's access to a wide range of foods, local and imported, often refined, processed and ready to eat.

Food suppliers and manufacturers bombard us with messages that do more to boost their sales than to promote your well-being. To add to the confusion, plenty of nutritional advice talks about 'healthy' choices – but 'healthy' food choices are not always weight loss food choices. Look twice at generalised messages put out to all shoppers; people have varying amounts of body fat and muscle mass, so some messages will be more suited to

'Healthy' food choices are not always weight loss food choices.

certain people than to others. It's similar to encouraging everyone to buy the same size shoe; it just won't fit all people!!

Different ethnicities often have quite distinct body makeups, and with more children from mixed-race relationships, body compositions now vary in a way that has never been seen before. No wonder there is no 'one size diet fits all' for weight loss.

Successful weight loss needs a little more knowledge and understanding. Let's get started! Put aside all those messages you've heard about healthy eating and good food choices. Forget about the long list of weight loss options on the market. Get ready to move away from diets and deprivation, and step into a new, fresh future that will have you losing and controlling your weight forever. Imagine a clean white canvas in front of you – that's what you're starting with.

Take a moment and ask yourself why you want to lose weight. Is it for the sake of your health? High blood pressure, high cholesterol, raised blood sugars, back pain, fertility, or arthritis in your lower joints – all respond very well to weight loss. Maybe you want improved energy levels. It's also fine if you simply want to feel better about yourself. Identifying your reasons will add strength to your decision to lose weight, and it's a decision that may be the most important one you ever make. You have decided to deal with a problem and the outcomes can only be good. Better sleep patterns, better energy, better self-esteem, and fewer visits to the doctor – the list just goes on and on and on!!

You don't have to share your decision or desire for your weight changes with anyone

> A diet designed for *every* body is not designed for *your* body.

else. Friends and family are not always as helpful as you would hope, and you may be disappointed with the 'support' you receive. What is important is that you see this is all about you. You've made the decision to make some very valuable changes to your life.

Cut the ties

It's tempting to offer you fast, big weight losses but there is no point in setting unrealistic goals. You want to enjoy yourself, have a life, and lose weight forever. You'll need to make changes, but to be sustainable and to give long-term results they will have to fit in with your lifestyle.

You'll have some habits that are comfortable for you, but don't suit your weight. You'll need to prepare yourself to let go of these routines, to cut the ties and to make some changes. Remind yourself that these are good changes, they'll free you from the burden of excess weight, so see them as a pleasure, not a chore. You can enjoy delicious meals, savour good food, pamper yourself by making time for exercise and lose the weight you want. New patterns at first may seem time consuming and slightly challenging, but as you settle into them and benefit from the results, it won't be long before they become your pattern of choice.

Find simple solutions

The old equation based on how much energy you take in (that's your food and fluid) compared with how much energy you use up (that's your activity and exercise) will always be important. But it's certainly not the whole story. It needs to be combined with understanding your body makeup to achieve the right balance for weight loss.

We are all unique: there may well be no one else in the world who is your gender, your age, your height, your weight, with the same body fat and muscle mass as you and who wants to lose weight. To move out of, and stay out of, the obesity epidemic sweeping the world, you'll need to align your food with your individual body makeup. But let's keep it simple. You don't need to count kilojoules or eat special foods. You can look forward to enjoying everyday foods from the supermarket, whether you are at home in your normal routine, away on holiday or eating out. It could just be a matter of adjusting your use of carbohydrates and proteins that makes all the difference.

So look ahead and feel good and positive about the exciting changes you are going to make. Be determined and believe in what you are doing!

> To succeed at losing weight, you need to understand YOU, before you focus on food.

> You can lose weight – with the right tools. Yes, simple and effective tools, so you know how to eat anything and everything and still control your weight.

Fuel yourself

You may feel you eat well, make healthy choices, and shouldn't have a weight problem. But if you are still searching for a solution, accept that some changes need to be made.

Remind yourself that food is your fuel. Putting food in your body is like putting petrol in your car. It provides you with energy and enables you to perform well. However, if you over-fuel yourself you'll gain weight. Fuelling to the correct level has become more difficult over the last 40 years with such easy access to food. Unlike the hunter-gatherer days when food was often difficult to find, you can now eat at any time and for all sorts of reasons that have nothing to do with a simple need for fuel. You may eat because you are bored, sad, anxious, happy, excited, stressed, or in pain; you may eat for comfort or to be sociable with friends and family who welcome you and offer hospitality with food and drinks.

As your body fat increases, your appetite also increases. That is when control over your weight starts to slip away and the unfortunate cycle of overeating (even maybe only slightly) kicks in. Effectively you'll be feeding, or fuelling, the wrong-sized person. However, as you take control and reduce your weight, your appetite will also reduce.

Some metabolic disorders and certain medications affect weight, but for most people weight control comes back to the 'energy in, energy out' equation. Less than 1% of the overweight population will have genetic reasons for extra weight. People may sometimes seem to have a family history with weight gain, but excess weight in different generations is more likely a result of food patterns that are passed down from parent to child.

Understanding how to fuel your body must go hand in hand with looking forward to and enjoying meals that are flavourful and have variety. Delicious tasting food helps to satisfy your appetite, so treat yourself to meat, chicken and fish that you enjoy, and to the freshest seasonal vegetables and fruit.

This is all about you and making food and exercise work for you.

You can lose weight – with the right tools. Yes, simple and effective tools, so you know how to eat anything and everything and still control your weight.

A busy lifestyle

Jane is 35 years old and happily married with 3 children – 6, 8 and 15 years. Her 15 year old daughter is from her former marriage. Jane works Monday to Thursday from 9.00am to 3.00pm. Her work days are mainly in front of a computer with a small amount of walking around the office to liaise with staff in different areas. Life is busy juggling work with family commitments; afternoons and evenings are taken up with transporting children to different activities, shopping, cooking and cleaning, which leaves little time for relaxation.

Jane enjoys cooking for the family although lack of time is often a problem. She feels she knows a reasonable amount about food and nutrition; however her weight has steadily increased since she had children. Her present weight is 87kgs but she remembers she was 68kgs before her first pregnancy. Jane says she cooks 'healthy' meals for the family and does try to get to yoga once a week along with at least one walk in the weekend. At a Doctor's appointment her blood pressure was slightly raised and tests showed her blood sugar levels were just above the normal range. It was noted she has a family history of diabetes. Her Doctor discussed her weight gain, and suggested she worked on turning this trend around. Jane was aware that her increasing weight could one day lead to health problems and was keen to avoid the need for medication.

She actioned the 'Size Does Matter' recommendations and 11 weeks later her weight has reduced to 79kgs. As well as feeling fabulous with better energy levels, her sweet tooth at the end of the day has gone and she notices she has improved control over her appetite. Jane enjoys her food and feels the changes she's made are sustainable and fit in well with her family and lifestyle.

At a recent follow-up visit with her Doctor, her blood pressure was normal and blood tests showed her blood sugars were reducing. With these health benefits, along with feeling so well, Jane is keen to continue with her weight loss.

2

Success for you

Turn the key
Providing energy
Refer to 'The Big Three'
Keep it simple with real food

Turn the key

Understanding more about the fat and muscle components of your body is the key to successful weight loss. Knowing how to link food to your body makeup is the only way forward to long-term weight control.

Your body uses energy all the time. Whether you are sleeping, sitting or moving around, your body requires energy (often called kilojoules) to function. Even when you are not moving, your body uses energy to keep your heart pumping, organs functioning and body temperature controlled.

The rate that your body uses energy is called your metabolic rate, and this is what determines how much food you need to eat to maintain, lose or gain weight.

The level of muscle in your body is a main factor in determining your metabolic rate. Muscle is active tissue and it uses energy or food at a faster rate than fat tissue. It is helpful to have a high muscle mass as this gives a higher metabolic rate, which requires and allows you to eat more. However, you need to know how to choose your food at meal times, otherwise a well-muscled person will feel hungrier sooner after eating than someone with less muscle. It is not uncommon to have a high muscle mass and a high body fat, and if you're in this situation you'll have a wonderful body makeup, once you've reduced your body fat.

Fat tissue, on the other hand, uses very little energy, and people who feel they 'only have to smell food to gain weight' will often have a low muscle mass and high body fat. If you are in this category you will need to be particular about portions. Once you have reduced your body fat, you could work on increasing your muscle mass to improve your metabolic rate.

If you are starting to feel that a standard set of scales is not particularly useful, you're probably right. From experience only 15% of clients can predict their body makeup successfully. The rest can be way off. Overweight clients are often surprised at how much muscle mass they carry and wonder how it got there. If you were active in your youth, you will still have that muscle. It's hard to lose, even as you gain fat. You will also develop more muscle as you carry extra body fat, and there are some people who are just born with a higher muscle mass.

So how do you find out what your body composition is? The answer lies with a body composition monitor. This technology is becoming more accessible. It uses a very small, harmless electric current to measure the varying bio-electric impedance as it passes through cells in the body. It can differentiate

> Knowing how to link food to your body makeup is essential – and the only way you will move ahead to long-term weight control.

When buying a body composition monitor, select one that shows how much fat and muscle you have, as well as your basal or resting metabolic rate.

between fat, muscle, fluid and bone. The sophistication of the technology is variable. Some equipment has sensors only for the feet, but the preferred technology has sensors for both the feet and the hands. Some dietitians, nutritionists, health practitioners and fitness centres will have this equipment. We have this technology at our Auckland office and it is available for public use (at a small charge). Visit www.weightwise.co.nz.

A domestic body composition monitor, available from retail outlets such as pharmacies, is not as accurate as the more advanced technology, but is certainly more helpful than a standard bathroom scale. When buying, select one that shows how much fat and muscle you have, as well as your basal or resting metabolic rate. (If you have difficulty sourcing a monitor with these specifications, they are available from www.weightwise.co.nz.)

With this type of technology becoming more readily available at a reasonable cost, it is only a matter of time before regular scales, with the clumsy and confusing information they give, become redundant.

BMI (Body Mass Index) is a measurement of total weight against height. The term is often used for assessing how overweight or obese someone is. But a BMI measurement is as limited as a measurement from a regular scale; it does not differentiate between fat and muscle, and extra muscle mass is interpreted as fat. For example, sports people often have a BMI that puts them in an obese range, but the truth is they have an excellent body composition, high in muscle and low in fat.

Once you know how much fat and muscle you have, you'll be able to make appropriate adjustments to your food choices, to put you on the path to appetite control and weight loss.

For your body makeup, we'll show you how to choose carbohydrates and proteins for best use of their energy so you get maximum fullness from a meal, and lose weight comfortably.

Refer to 'The Big Three'

To lose weight, three factors need to support each other

- Your food
- Your fluid
- Your exercise

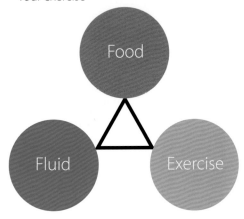

Providing energy

At this stage we should clarify the use of the word 'energy'. Food provides your body with energy. This energy is needed to keep your body moving and functioning in many ways. The amount of energy that food provides is measured in kilojoules. (In some countries, energy is measured in calories, which is an abbreviation for kilocalories. To enable you to compare, one calorie is equivalent to 4.2 kilojoules.)

Over the years, food has been analysed a great deal. Scientists know how much protein, fat and carbohydrate just about every food contains and therefore how many kilojoules the food provides to you. This information is readily available in 'calorie counting' books. For years people have counted the kilojoules in their diet in an attempt to lose weight but unfortunately, without a great deal of success.

While you are losing weight you will regularly refer to this trio of factors and check the balance between them. It's an easy way of assessing your progress as you make changes. All three factors work together for improved appetite control and easier weight loss. The exercise and fluid give you great support by helping you to identify when you are full; they keep you focused and feeling positive along with good energy levels. But without a doubt food has the biggest potential to dictate your weight loss progress.

An encouraging part of weight loss is that as your weight reduces, so will your appetite. You often don't need to lose a lot of weight to start noticing the change in your appetite.

Keep it simple with real food

Weight loss is not about putting a good or a bad label on foods, and depriving yourself never brings successful long-term weight loss. Far more effective is learning how *all* foods can work for you.

To do this you'll need some simple messages about carbohydrates, proteins and fats. Everything you eat can be put into one of these three general categories. As some foods fit into more than one category, they will be put into the category that is the most helpful for weight loss. Carbohydrates and proteins supply energy to you at different rates. For your body makeup, we'll show you how to choose carbohydrates and proteins for best use of their energy so you get maximum fullness from a meal, and lose weight comfortably.

It's a bit like understanding the difference between shampoo, toothpaste and soap. They all clean the body, but are used in different ways. You don't have to think about which cleaner to use on your teeth. You'll soon become just as familiar with carbohydrates, proteins and fats when making suitable food choices.

At the end of the chapters on carbohydrates, proteins, fats and fluids, you will find Unit lists, where the foods and fluids are in portions of a similar kilojoule value. These are to help you visualise suitable portions and to give you flexibility with choices.

> An encouraging part of weight loss is that as your weight reduces, so will your appetite. You often don't need to lose a lot of weight to start noticing the change in your appetite.

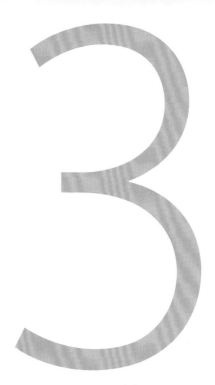

Carbs are on the menu

About carbohydrate

Over the years, carbohydrates have been tossed around, frowned at, and sometimes even banned, as different diets – the low carb, the no carb, the no carb in the evening, and even the low GI carb – made their various appearances. Treated so warily by diet authors, the media and consumers alike, no wonder they are often thought of as a problem food.

To add to this confusion, carbohydrates are easy to come by. Improved technology has enabled more processing and this has increased the range of convenient snack products available. Carbohydrates keep well in packets at room temperature and can be readily stored in cupboards or carried in bags and pockets. But the processing has often removed fibre from the food, and even though the promise of low fat may be stamped on the packaging, don't be mislead by this as those quick snacks certainly provide kilojoules, without necessarily giving a feeling of fullness.

Carbohydrates are less expensive than proteins, and often turn up in oversized portions. For a small extra cost to themselves, lunch bars may use large bread rolls or thicker slices of bread in their sandwiches to help persuade their customers that they are getting good value. Unfortunately, the apparent 'generosity' is just another factor pushing your weight up. Rice and pasta, too, have become the star performers in a meal rather than mere side players. Next time you are out for an Italian or Asian-style meal, take note of how much pasta or rice is put on your plate – it's usually a generous serving.

Energy from carbohydrate

The main function of carbohydrates is to provide energy (or fuel) for the body. When you eat a carbohydrate, the process of digestion starts fairly quickly. Blood sugar levels soon rise, improving your energy level and satisfying your appetite. The energy from carbohydrates will last around 2 – 2 ½ hours, at which point your blood sugar levels start to drop, and you may notice you feel tired, or hungry, or both. Carbohydrates with higher fibre will last closer to 2 ½ hours, whereas processed and refined foods with less fibre may only help you for an hour or so.

As your percentage of body fat increases, so too does your appetite. In addition, the more muscle mass you have, the higher your metabolic rate, and the faster you use carbohydrates. So if you have a high body fat and a high muscle mass, the carbohydrates you eat during a meal may hold your blood sugars up and provide you with fuel for only 1 ½ – 2 hours – at which stage you start looking for food or feeling tired. This is why, while you are losing weight, carbohydrate should be included at each meal, but not constitute the entire meal, as you will not feel full enough for long enough.

Over the last 40 years the number of malnourished people and overweight people in the world has totally reversed. This reversal began at the same time as breakfast cereals were introduced. A coincidence? Maybe not. Sure, our lifestyles have changed. Forty years ago, we still had to get up to change the TV channel, and

Eat as much as you like of the 'unrestricted' vegetables

our pantries weren't so easily stocked with such an array of tempting treats, but it's still interesting to wonder if adopting the cereal habit – which gave breakfast a mainly carbohydrate profile, whereas the traditional eggs or baked beans on toast had given it a blend of carbohydrate and protein – has helped to make us hungrier over the day and consequently pushed weights up.

Sources of carbohydrate

The main sources of carbohydrates are breakfast cereals, breads, cakes, biscuits, crackers, snack bars, rice, pasta, noodles, vegetables, fruits and sugars.

Breakfast cereals: There's a huge selection on the market and most are promoted in a manner that would have you believe they are a perfect product for you. They can be high in fibre and low in fat, but do they keep you feeling full for long enough?

Breads and bread products: A brown or grain bread is a better choice as the fibre will help give you more fullness. In recent years some of the newer breads are sliced generously. Women, especially, should opt for the thinner slice of sandwich bread. One slice of bread from a bakery loaf or a domestic bread maker is usually equivalent to almost 2 sandwich slices from a commercial loaf.

On the whole, the heavier, denser breads are higher in kilojoules. The thin wraps look as if they should be a better choice; however, they often contain all

the kilojoules but without the raising agent. Although a bagel is low in fat, they are dense items and, typically, one bagel is equivalent to 3 or 4 sandwich slices of bread.

Cakes and biscuits: If they're in front of you, why wouldn't you eat them? Check your access to these foods and keep them in the freezer, or bake items for the family that don't appeal to you so much. Successful weight loss will never be about deprivation so it's not that you can't have them at all, but do ask yourself if they're a good enough choice for you on your weight loss journey!

Crackers: The amount of fat in crackers varies considerably. Check the 'per100g serve' column on the Nutrition Information Panel on the label and choose a cracker with fat levels of 8g per 100g or lower. Crackers are interesting because they offer variety with their crunchy texture, but they also have a sneaky way of escaping from the packet and into your hands, when really you only wanted a couple. It's often all those little extras that have led to your weight gain. Remember, it's not only the cracker you need to consider; it's what you put on it as well.

Snack bars: Often packaged with a health message, however typically these are equivalent to almost 2 sandwich slices of bread.

Rice, pasta, noodles: Choose products you enjoy. If you like brown rice or wholemeal

This = that
carbohydrate portions

Pita bread ⅔ small

Rice, white, cooked ½ cup

Bread roll ½ small

Bread 1 medium slice

Cereal bar ½

Marshmallows 6

Croissant ⅓

Gingernuts 1 ½

Bagel ¼

These foods are all in portions of a similar kilojoule value, and for simplicity can be described as 1 UNIT.

pasta, that's great, as they will increase your feeling of fullness. But if you prefer white rice, then have it. You need to make choices that taste good to you. Rice, pasta and noodles are all cheap, easy foods and it's easy for portions to be oversized. Crispy noodles have been deep fried, so will be higher in kilojoules.

Vegetables: There are the starchy vegetables that contain kilojoules, and there are those that are often referred to as 'free' or 'unrestricted' as they contain very few kilojoules. Vegetables are dietary heroes, because they offer great health benefits and they all contain fibre, which helps you to feel full. Choose from as wide a range as possible, with different shades of greens, yellows, oranges and reds included.

The kilojoule-containing vegetables include potatoes, kumara, pumpkin, parsnips, corn, taro, yams and beetroot.

The 'free' or 'unrestricted' vegetable category includes asparagus, Asian greens, sprouts, broccoli, Brussels sprouts, carrots, courgettes, cucumber, cabbage, capsicums, cauliflower, celery, egg plant, garlic, ginger, green beans, all fresh herbs, leeks, lettuce, mushrooms, onion, parsley, radish, rocket, silver beet, snow peas, spinach, spring onions, tomato, swedes, turnips and watercress. On their own they won't make a meal, but in conjunction with carbohydrate and protein they will definitely help with fullness. The good amount of fibre they offer also involves more chewing, which adds to the satisfaction a meal will give you. Eat as much as you like of these 'unrestricted'

vegetables. Fresh, frozen or tinned versions are all fine. Welcome them in and make them taste good, so you'll want more. (Check the recipes in Ch 13 for ideas.)

Fruits: Fruits are often mistakenly thought of as belonging to the same category as the 'unrestricted' vegetables. But both fresh and tinned fruits do come with kilojoules from their natural sugar content and for weight loss usually a maximum of 1 – 2 servings per day is recommended. If using tinned fruit, choose product in juice and then drain and discard the juice. In another example of a generalised message about healthy food choices that can be very misleading for anyone wanting to lose weight, dried fruit is often promoted as a healthy snack. Don't be deceived, as even though the fluid has been removed, the sugar is still present. Dried fruits are small, but dense in kilojoules. They're a fine snack for active people, but not a good choice when you want to lose weight.

Sugars: This category includes white sugar, brown sugar, honey, jams, jellies, sweets, cordials, fruit juices, vegetable juices and sweetened drinks. These foods have empty kilojoules in that they have the kilojoules but provide very little nutritional value. It's worth noting white sugar, brown sugar and honey are all similar in kilojoules.

Artificial sweeteners

Your food needs to taste good to you. If you are happy with an artificial sweetener,

This = that
carbohydrate portions

Weetbix 1 ½

Sushi 2 rounds

Instant noodles ¼ packet

Pinky bar ½

Shapes 7-8

Brown sugar 2 tbsp

Honey 1 tbsp

White sugar 2 tbsp

These foods are all in portions of a similar kilojoule value, and for simplicity can be described as 1 UNIT.

This = that
carbohydrate portions

Pizza base ⅙

Rice crackers 12

Litebreads 3

Toffee pop 1

Cornflakes ⅔ cup

Kumara ½ cup

Potato ½ cup

Apple – medium 1

These foods are all in portions of a similar kilojoule value, and for simplicity can be described as 1 UNIT.

Apricots – dried 8

Prunes 4

Banana ½

Blueberries ⅔ cup

Chocolate 2 squares

Le Snak 1

Orange 1

Ryvita 2

It's interesting to wonder if adopting the cereal habit – which gave breakfast a mainly carbohydrate profile, whereas the traditional eggs or baked beans on toast had given it a blend of carbohydrate and protein – has helped to make us hungrier over the day and consequently pushed weights up.

then go ahead and use it. If you prefer sugar and are able to keep the amount low, then choose sugar.

You may decide to use artificial sweeteners as a temporary measure while your weight loss gets underway and go back to using sugar moderately once you are confident with managing your weight.

Glycaemic index

Glycaemic index (GI) has been given a great deal of attention in recent years. GI is a measure of how fast a food is broken down and therefore how fast it will affect your blood sugar levels. A high glycaemic index food is digested and absorbed quickly and does not satisfy you for long, whereas a low glycaemic index food is more slowly digested and therefore satisfies you for longer.

There is certainly no harm in choosing low glycaemic index foods; however, they are not a strong factor in successful weight loss. You'll still need to understand what a suitable portion is, as low GI foods are not lower in kilojoules. For example, some of the low GI breads from bakeries are the highest kilojoule breads on the market.

Rather than looking at individual foods, look at the combination of foods in your meal or snack. By including a carbohydrate and a protein, the glycaemic index is reduced significantly and this will make you feel fuller for longer.

GLYCAEMIC INDEX (GI) TABLE

Low GI (<55)	Medium GI (55-70)	High GI (>70)
Breads Multigrain bread, special low GI white bread, sour dough bread, pumpernickel bread	Hamburger bun, croissant, light rye, crumpet, pita bread, French baguette (traditional), buckwheat bread	White bread, gluten free bread, bagels, wholemeal bread, waffles
Breakfast Cereals & Grains All-bran, porridge made from rolled oats, toasted muesli Barley, pasta, noodles, bulgur wheat, quinoa, buckwheat	Muesli-non toasted, muesli bars, wheat flakes, Weetbix Basmati rice, Arborio rice	Bran flakes, cornflakes, rice bubbles Jasmine fragrant rice, white rice, brown rice
Fruit & Starchy Vegetables Apple, dried apricot, banana, grapefruit, mango, orange, peach, pear, plum, cherries, grapes, canned peaches in juice Baked beans, chickpeas	Fresh/canned apricots, paw paw, pineapple, rock melon, sultanas, canned peaches in syrup, kiwifruit Potato (white with skin, baked), beetroot	Watermelon, dates Potato (white without skin, baked), broad beans, pumpkin, kumara, fries
Dairy Foods Milk, soy milk, custard, low fat fruit yoghurt, diet yoghurt, low fat ice cream	Full cream ice cream	
Biscuits/Snack Foods Apple muffins made with rolled oats, sponge cake, popcorn – plain cooked in microwave	Digestive biscuits, milk arrowroot biscuits, blueberry muffins, rye crackers with oats or sesame seeds, potato crisps, popcorn – plain cooked in microwave with butter	Water crackers, corn thins, crispbread, pretzels

Note: The GI may change depending on cooking method, variety and brand.

This = that carbohydrate units

The following foods are all in portions of a similar kilojoule value, and for simplicity can be described as 1 UNIT. For example 1 round crumpet (under breads) is 1 UNIT and has similar kilojoules to 1½ ginger nuts (under biscuits, baked items), which is also 1 UNIT. In other words this = that as every item on the list is 1 UNIT. This is to help you get a feel for portions that are suitable for you when you are choosing and designing your meals and snacks.

Abbreviations: tsp = teaspoon, tbsp = tablespoon

Breads	Serving Size
Bread (wheatmeal/multigrain)	1 med slice
Bread roll (mixed grain)	½ small
Crumpet (round)	1
Fruit muffin	⅓
Croissant	⅓
English muffin split	½
Hamburger bun	⅓
Pita bread	⅓ medium
Pita bread	⅔ small
Bagel	¼
Fruit bread	1 thick slice
Wrap-rectangle	¼
Chapatti	⅔
Panini	¼
Fruit bun	½
Burrito tortilla	½
Pizza Base (23cm base)	⅙

Crackers	Serving Size
Ryvita	2
Litebread	3
Carrs water crackers	6
Vita wheat	3
Rice wafers	2
Rice snacks	12
Saladas (low fat)	1 ½
Cruskitts	4
Kavali	5
Huntley & Palmer cream crackers	2

Biscuits/Baked items	Serving Size
Gingernuts	1 ½
Mallow puff	1
Toffee pop	1
Pikelets	1 ½

Cereals	Serving Size
All Bran	½ cup
Just Right	½ cup
Light'n'Tasty	½ cup
Rolled oats – raw	¼ cup
Special K	⅔ cup
Corn flakes	⅔ cup
Weetbix	1 ½
Cooked porridge (with water)	⅔ cup
Cooked porridge (with milk)	¼ cup

Pasta/Noodles	Serving Size
Pasta	½ cup
Noodles	½ cup
Spaghetti – tinned in tomato sauce	½ cup
Instant noodles	¼ packet
Noodles in a pot	¼ pot

Grains	Serving size
Rice – white (cooked)	½ cup
Rice – brown (cooked)	⅓ cup
Couscous – cooked, no added fat	½ cup
Flour – wheat	3 tbsp level
Sushi	2 rounds

Snacks	Serving Size	Fruits	Serving Size
Popcorn, lightly buttered	2 ½ cups	Apple – medium	1
Le Snak	1	Apricots	3
Cereal bar	½	Apricots – dried 1/2s	8
Pinky bar (45g)	½	Banana	½
Corn chips	⅔ cup	Blueberries	⅔ cup
Iceblock	1	Cherries	1 cup
Marshmallows	6	Cherries – glace	6
Chocolate	2 squares	Dates – dried	3
Grain Waves	½ cup	Feijoas	4
Potato crisps	½ cup	Figs – fresh	3
Pita Crispbreads	½ cup	Fruit salad – fresh	⅓ cup
Pretzels	½ cup	Grapefruit	1
Shapes	7 – 8	Grapes	½ cup
Muesli bar yoghurt coated	½	Kiwifruit	1 ½
Fruit leather	⅔	Melon	1 cup
Licorice	2 cm x 15cm	Watermelon	1 ½ cups
Sugar	**Serving Size**	Nectarines – small	2
Sugar white	2 tbsp	Orange	1
Sugar brown	2 tbsp	Peach	1
Golden syrup	1 ½ tbsp	Peaches in juice (drained)	⅔ cup
Honey	1 tbsp	Pear	1
Jam	2 tbsp	Pear – Nashi	1
Starchy Vegetables	**Serving Size**	Pears in juice (drained)	⅔ cup
Beetroot	6 slices	Pineapple – fresh	¾ cup
Broadbeans	⅔ cup	Plums	2
Corn	½ cup	Prunes	4
Frozen vegies – carrots/corn/peas	⅔ cup	Raspberries	1 cup
Kumara	½ cup	Strawberries	1 cup
Parsnip & Carrot mash	½ cup	Sultanas	2 tbsp – level
Peas	⅔ cup	Tamarillos	2
Potato	½ cup	Tangelo	1
Pumpkin	¾ cup	Fruit pot	1
Carrot	1 ½ cups		
Taro	½ cup		
Yam	½ cup		

4

The power of protein

About protein
Energy from protein
Sources of protein
Choices for you
This = that protein units

About protein

Protein is possibly the most underestimated food for successful weight loss. There's power to protein, and you need to know how to use it.

Proteins are made up of amino acids, which are important building blocks in the body and a component of all cells. There are some amino acids that your body needs but cannot produce, and you rely on your food to provide these. This is why protein must be included in your diet. Luckily, you live in a country that produces a treasure trove of excellent protein. Delicious varieties of meat, poultry, fish, cheese, eggs, milk and yoghurt are readily available, and now it's just a matter of getting them to work for you.

Energy from protein

Because proteins are complex molecules, it takes the body longer to break them down. It may take 2 – 2 ½ hours after eating them before they are available to give you their energy-raising benefits. That's why proteins work very well with carbohydrates. Carbohydrates give you energy almost immediately. That energy can last up to 2 – 2 ½ hours before you start to feel hungry or tired. At that point the protein included in your meal becomes available to pick up your blood sugar levels and energy levels, which will satisfy your appetite and carry you through to the next meal. With protein providing this back-up energy, the meal you ate keeps you satisfied for longer and you will find you have better appetite control. As noted in the previous chapter, a higher body fat will make you hungrier and the use of carbohydrate with protein will help by sustaining you for longer. Plus, the higher your muscle mass and metabolic rate, the faster you will use carbohydrate, so the more helpful this inclusion of protein will be.

Research reveals the benefits of including protein at a meal, for improved appetite control. It's worth considering the different breakfasts from around the world. Traditionally, northern Europeans breakfast on breads and sliced meats, cheeses and hard boiled eggs; Asians customarily select congee (rice with meat); Indians habitually opt for rice with curried meat. All these breakfasts consist of carbohydrate and protein – and the inhabitants of these countries do not have the weight issues seen in many of the countries that have a predominantly carbohydrate breakfast of cereal, fruit, and toast with jam or honey (see chart Obesity Rates in the World page 39).

As with all good stories, there's a catch. This is not about eating lots of protein because if you eat more than you need, the excess will be broken down and stored as fat. The moral of the story is to redistribute your protein intake over the day.

Sources of protein

Proteins are classified as either animal or vegetable.

Animal protein foods are meat, poultry, fish, seafood, eggs, and dairy products such as cheese, milk and yoghurt.

Meat, poultry, fish, seafood and cheese contain approximately 20 – 25% protein.

Obesity Rates in the World

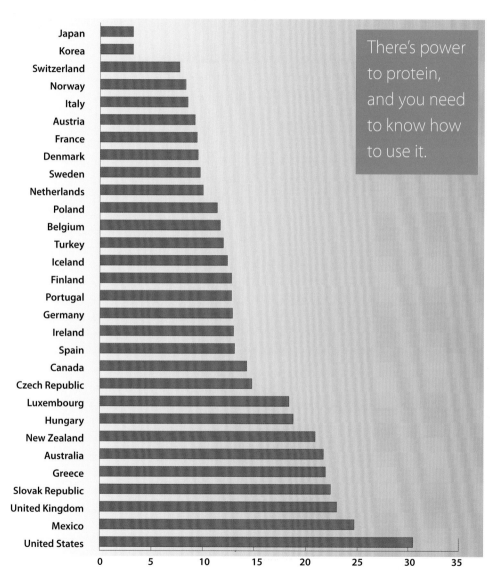

There's power to protein, and you need to know how to use it.

Percentages of total population (aged 15 and older) classified as obese

Source: OECD Health data 2005

Eggs are around 13% protein and milk and yoghurt between 4 – 10% protein. The lower protein content of milk and yoghurt makes dairy products perfect as a snack, rather than as the main protein source of a meal. Dairy items are sometimes overlooked in weight loss plans, but they shouldn't be. They are a useful snack in that they provide carbohydrate plus protein, and are also an excellent source of calcium. What's more, there is a factor in dairy items that allows your body to excrete more fat. So don't leave them out. Include them and make them work for you.

Animal sources of proteins are often called 'complete' proteins as they provide all the amino acids our bodies require.

Vegetable protein foods are legumes e.g. lentils, chickpeas, split peas, beans; tofu and soy products; whole grains e.g. rice, pasta, breads, cereals; and nuts and seeds. Legumes and whole grains contain 5 – 10% protein, soy products contain 6 – 8 % protein and nuts and seeds are 15 – 25% protein.

Apart from soy products, vegetable proteins are called 'incomplete' proteins, as they do not contain all of the required amino acids. To be well nourished when using only vegetarian sources of protein, you need to consume a wide variety daily.

Understanding the considerable differences in the protein content of various food sources will help you with your food choices during weight loss. You may have identified that foods with higher amounts of protein keep you feeling fuller for longer. Interestingly, well-muscled people are often very fond of their meat, chicken and fish and may consume 2 – 3 times their requirement at the evening meal. Unsurprisingly, they may also be overweight.

Choices for you

Protein foods contain varying levels of fats and oils and choosing lower-fat varieties will help your weight loss. Select well-trimmed cuts of meat. By all means cook your chicken with the skin on as it keeps it moist, however be aware that the fat sits just under the skin. Fresh and smoked salmon are farmed fish and contain higher levels of fat (between 15 – 34%) than tinned salmon, which is an ocean fish and has less fat (usually around 8%). White fleshed fish and seafood are suitable protein options. Cheeses need to be used very carefully. Many cheeses promoted as low fat are not as low as you would hope. For example, cheeses marketed as having 25% less fat than cheddar cheese still contain about 25% fat, and this is double the fat level of other proteins such as meat and poultry. If you haven't tried cottage cheese for a couple of years and didn't like it the last time, try it again. It's improved a lot. Use the regular rather than low-fat option as it has a thicker texture and is still low fat! Nuts, seeds and nut butters are all about 50% fat so forget about those healthy food choice messages and ask yourself if they are good enough for you at the moment.

Remember, it's not about deprivation. It's not that you can't have these higher-fat options, but as you're looking for weight loss, you may want to put them aside just for a while.

This = that
protein portions

Ham 50g

Beef mince 40g

Lentils ½ cup

Beef steak 50g

White fish 65g

Crumbed frozen fish ½

Tofu ½ cup

Shrimps ⅔ cup

These foods are all in portions of a similar kilojoule value, and for simplicity can be described as 1 UNIT.

This = that
protein portions

Tinned salmon 70g

Cottage cheese ⅓ cup

Egg 1

Chicken 1 drumstick

Sausage ½

Smoked salmon 30g

Milk – trim 190mls

42

These foods are all in portions of a similar kilojoule value, and for simplicity can be described as 1 UNIT.

Milk –dark blue 125mls

Edam cheese 24g

Cheddar cheese 22g

Parmesan cheese 3 tbsp

Feta cheese 32g

Yoghurt 150g ½ pot

Baked beans ⅓ cup

This = that protein units

The following foods are all in portions of a similar kilojoule value, and for simplicity can be described as 1 UNIT.

Weights are after cooking by a low fat method.
Abbreviations: tsp = teaspoon, tbsp = tablespoon

Meat	Serving Size
Steak	50g
Sausage	½
Beef mince	40g
Lamb steak	60g
Lamb cutlet	2 small
Eyes of bacon (medallions)	4
Frankfurter	½
Ham	50g
Ham steak	½
Luncheon	1 ½ slices
Pork	70g
Venison	75g
Liver – lamb	40g (9cm x 5cm x 1cm)
Kidneys – lamb	2 whole
Black pudding	1 slice (4cm x 2cm diam)
Pate – pork	2 tbsp – level
Salami	3 thin slices (5cm diam)
Beef jerky	25g (½ of a snack pack)
Poultry	**Serving Size**
Thighs	40g (½ or ⅓)
Breast (single)	50g (⅓)
Drumsticks	1
Egg	1
Fish and Seafood	**Serving Size**
White fish	65g
Salmon – fresh	25g
Salmon – smoked	30g
Salmon – tinned	70g (⅔ tin)

Sardines	½ tin (55g)
Fish fingers	2
Tuna – tinned – in brine/springwater	75g
Paua	1 average
Mussels – steamed	½ cup
Oysters – natural	½ cup
Shrimps – prawns	⅔ cup
Crabmeat/surimi	⅔ cup
Legumes/ Pulses/ Vegetarian	**Serving Size**
Tofu	½ cup (90g)
Lentils	½ cup
Chickpea	½ cup
Beans red kidney	½ cup
Hummus	⅓ cup
Baked beans	⅓ cup
Vegetable sausage	¾
Dairy	**Serving Size**
Cheddar cheese	22g
Cream cheese	1 ½ tbsp (level)
Lite cream cheese	2 tbsp (level)
Camembert/Brie	¼ small round
Edam	24g
Feta	32g
Cheese slices – reduced fat	2 slices
Parmesan cheese	3 tbsp
Ricotta	4 tbsp
Milk – Dark blue	125mls
Milk – Trim	190mls
Milk – Calcitrim	165mls
Flavoured milk	125mls
Soy milk	125mnls
Lite soy milk	165 mls
Yoghurt pot (150g)	½ pot
Ice cream – vanilla	⅓ cup
Sour cream	2 ½ tbsp (level)
Lite sour cream	4 tbsp (level)
Cottage cheese	⅓ cup
Lite cottage cheese	½ cup

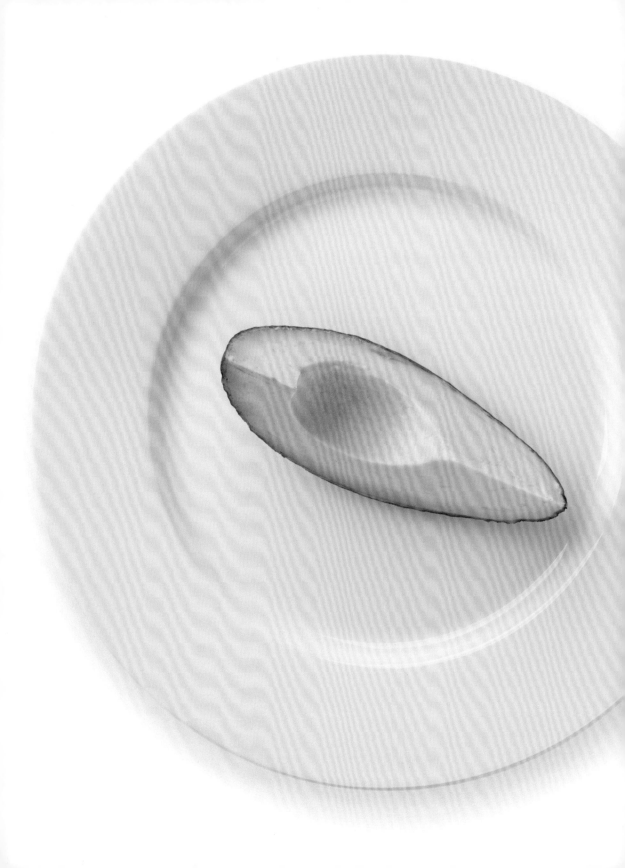

Get fickle with your fats

About fat and oil

It's easy to be confused by all the mixed messages surrounding fats and oils. What really are 'good' fats and oils and 'bad' fats and oils, and if avocado, fresh salmon, seeds and nuts are all 'good' fats, why shouldn't they be eaten often and in plentiful amounts? This labelling of 'good' and 'bad' has nothing to do with the kilojoule value of food. Both 'good' and 'bad' fats and oils are all high in kilojoules, so those avocadoes, salmon, seeds and nuts will put weight on you at a rate that doesn't seem fair!

The 'good' and the 'bad'

How did this 'good' and 'bad' labelling come about? To explain, fats can be classified as saturated and unsaturated.

Saturated fats are mainly animal fats. They include butter, cheese, cream, lard, fat in milk, fat on meats and any products containing them, such as salamis, pates and sausages. The only plant foods that contain saturated fat are palm oil and coconut oil. These oils are usually not found in the supermarket, but are used in the commercial manufacture of biscuits, cakes, pastries and other snack foods.

Saturated fats should be kept to a minimum as they interfere with heart health and have been shown to be a factor in raised blood cholesterol levels. This is the reason they are labelled as 'bad' fats. With regard to your weight, saturated fats are all high kilojoule foods and therefore need to be used sparingly.

Unsaturated fats consist of monounsaturated and polyunsaturated fats. Monounsaturated fats are found easily in a range of foods. They

Monounsaturated and polyunsaturated fats are high in kilojoules and, like saturated fats, need to be used carefully for successful weight loss.

are in milk products, nuts and seeds, vegetable oils, avocado and fatty fish. If necessary, our body is able to make monounsaturated fats. Polyunsaturated fats are different. They must come from the diet, and are essential to make a variety of hormones and to make cell walls. There are two types of polyunsaturated fats, omega 6 and omega 3. Omega 6 fats are found in nuts and seeds, vegetable oils and table spreads, and omega 3 fats are in fatty fish such as sardines, tuna, salmon, herrings and mussels and vegetable oils. Fish is a potent source of omega 3 and is the reason for the recommendation of 2 serves of fish per week. The unsaturated fats have been shown to help with heart health by reducing blood cholesterol levels and this is why they are labelled as 'good' fats. With regard to your weight however, monounsaturated and polyunsaturated fats are high in kilojoules and, like saturated fats, need to be used carefully for successful weight loss.

You may have heard of trans fats, which are found in processed products such as margarines. They are unsaturated, but behave like saturated fats and are not good for heart health. Food manufacturers are making a good effort to keep trans fats as low as possible or to remove them all together, which is helpful for your weight loss as they are also high in kilojoules.

This=that
fat and oil portions

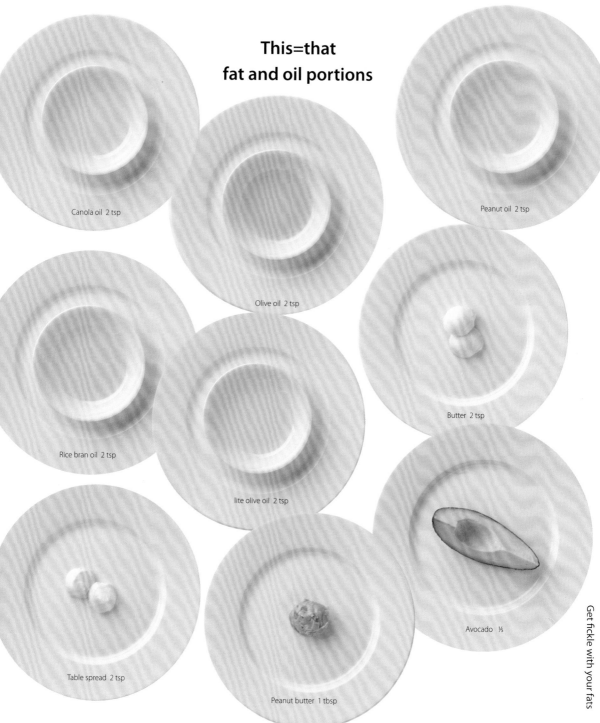

Canola oil 2 tsp

Olive oil 2 tsp

Peanut oil 2 tsp

Rice bran oil 2 tsp

lite olive oil 2 tsp

Butter 2 tsp

Table spread 2 tsp

Peanut butter 1 tbsp

Avocado ⅕

These foods are all in portions of a similar kilojoule value, and for simplicity can be described as 1 UNIT.

> Both 'good' and 'bad' fats and oils are all high in kilojoules, so those avocadoes, salmon, seeds and nuts will put weight on you at a rate that doesn't seem fair!

still having enjoyable, delicious meals.

Keep an eye out for hidden sources of fats and oils. They lurk in foods such as muffins, cakes, biscuits, doughnuts, sausage rolls, pies, fresh salmon, smoked salmon, chocolate, snack foods, corn chips, potato crisps, crispy noodles, pesto, tapenade, dips, mayonnaise, salad dressings, all seeds and nuts, peanut butter, avocado, desiccated coconut, and fried and takeaway foods. Fats are everywhere in your diet, and because they are so dense in kilojoules, they can have a huge impact on your weight.

The nature of the beast

The message about choosing foods that are low in fats and oils for weight loss has been around for years. It's a good message because, as the densest source of kilojoules in your diet, fats and oils affect your weight easily. One gram of fat or oil provides 37 kilojoules; one gram of protein or carbohydrate provides 16 – 17 kilojoules. Weight for weight, fats and oils provide about double the kilojoules of other foods.

They can slide into our food very easily without being identified. For instance, if you were out for brunch and chose scrambled eggs, you would have no idea how much butter or cream the chef had used. It's the same with mashed potatoes – difficult to know how much fat is added for flavour. Oil doesn't make food look any bigger, but it certainly throws the kilojoules up high.

Meals that are too low in fat become tasteless, and difficult to chew and swallow, as they are dry. So for weight loss you'll need to find a happy balance between keeping these kilojoule-dense foods as low as possible and

Getting smart with choices

Small smart changes in your use of fats and oils on a regular basis can help considerably with weight control. Success will build its own momentum; as your weight and appetite reduce, it will become easier to make lower-fat choices. It's the opposite process from one you may have noticed in your earlier days, when, as your body weight increased, you were almost inevitably drawn to higher-fat choices in your food.

When using butter or table spread, use it sparingly – scrape it on and scrape it off. That's a very good habit to develop for the rest of your life. Use oil sparingly in cooking, too, putting a little in the pan and wiping it out with a paper towel, even when using spray oil. Choose well-trimmed cuts of meat. Premium grade mince and quality sausages are fine. Casseroles are a good cooking method, as the fat comes to the surface during cooking and can be skimmed off. Barbecues are ideal when you use the grill plate rather than the solid plate, allowing fat to drip away. Similarly, roasts should be cooked on a rack. If you want to use the juices to make gravy, skim the fat off the surface, then thicken and add water or vegetable water. Packet gravies may be used as they are all low in fats.

For fresh fish choose a white fish or tuna, and use oil carefully when cooking. Check the label on tinned fish;10g or less of fat per 100g of fish would be a good choice. Tinned salmon is an ocean salmon and is much lower in fat than the fresh and smoked salmon which are farmed.

Try mashing your potatoes with milk and, rather than adding butter, use finely chopped parsley, onion or herbs for flavouring. Vegetables can be stir fried with less oil and a little stock or soy sauce. Roast vegetables need to be cooked in a separate dish from the meat. Put a little oil on your hands and rub it onto the vegetables. To brown them, use the fan bake function in your oven. This is also a good method for cooking your own wedges. Dressings add delicious flavour to a salad. You could use balsamic vinegar, or there are plenty of good 'lite' or low-kilojoule dressings on the market. The 'lite' mayonnaises are usually not as light in kilojoules as you would hope.

Filo pastry is a great alternative to other pastry, and you can use milk instead of oil to layer it up.

Use cheese as a seasoning, sparingly, for taste. Cottage cheese is a low-fat option. The regular product has a firmer texture and would be quite acceptable. There's a large range of milks on the market. Lite blue or lower in fat would be a good choice.

How light is 'lite'?

'Lite' is probably not as light as you would hope. 'Lite' olive oil, for example, has the same kilojoule count as regular olive oil. In this case, the word 'lite' refers to flavour rather than kilojoules. During the process of obtaining oil, olives are initially cold pressed to give a very good quality, flavourful oil such as extra virgin. Then the olives are heated and given a second pressing. This produces a less flavourful oil which is called 'lite'. Next time you are at the supermarket, have a look at the Nutrition Information Panel on the label. You will notice the energy per 100g for the regular and the 'lite' olive oils are similar.

The word 'lite' on a label can give the impression a food may be used in unrestricted amounts. By all means use them, but keep in mind that the 'lite' versions of mayonnaise, cream cheese, sour cream, ice cream and table spread will not have a significantly lower kilojoule count than their full-fat counterparts, so you'll still need to take care of portion sizes. 'Lite' dressings are a good choice as they have had all or most of the oil taken out.

These two portions have a similar kilojoule value.

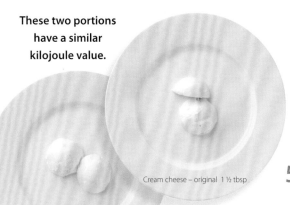

Cream cheese – original 1 ½ tbsp

Cream cheese – lite 2 tbsp

This = that
fat and oil portions

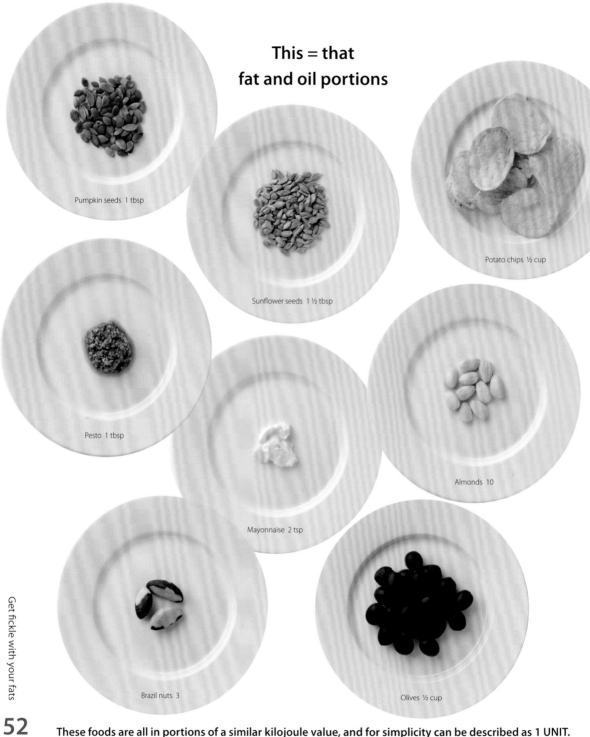

Pumpkin seeds 1 tbsp

Sunflower seeds 1 ½ tbsp

Potato chips ½ cup

Pesto 1 tbsp

Mayonnaise 2 tsp

Almonds 10

Brazil nuts 3

Olives ½ cup

These foods are all in portions of a similar kilojoule value, and for simplicity can be described as 1 UNIT.

This = that fat and oil units

The following foods are all in portions of a similar kilojoule value, and for simplicity can be described as 1 UNIT.

Abbreviations: tsp = teaspoon, tbsp = tablespoon

Oils and Fats	Serving Size
Oil (eg olive/canola/sunflower)	2 tsp
Butter	2 tsp
Table spread	2 tsp
Proactiv	3 tsp
Beef dripping	2 tsp
Fries (McDonalds)	½ small
Spring roll (deep fried)	½
Sausage roll	5cm
Coconut cream	2 tbsp
Coconut cream (lite)	⅔ cup
Ricotta cheese	4 tbsp
Peanut butter	1 tbsp
Avocado	⅕
Pesto	1 tbsp
Parmesan	3 tbsp
Tahini	2 tsp
Pine nuts	1 ½ tbsp
Pumpkin seeds	1 tbsp
Sunflower seeds	1 ½ tbsp
Sesame seeds	1 ½ tbsp
Coconut – desiccated	2 tbsp
Potato crisps	½ cup
Corn chips	⅔ cup
Mayonnaise	2 tsp
Salad cream	1 ½ tbsp
Vinaigrette	1 tbsp
Olives	½ cup
Cream	1 ½ tbsp
Hazelnuts	1 ½ tbsp
Cashew nuts	9 to 10
Almonds	10
Walnuts	2 ½
Brazil nuts	3
Macadamia nuts	3

Hungry or thirsty?

Water, water everywhere but . . .
Like it hot?
What about juices and energy drinks?
Alcohol
Suitable options
This = that alcohol and fluid units

Water, water everywhere but . . .

A hungry person may, in fact, just be a thirsty person. Yes, hunger and thirst are easily confused. The first symptom of not drinking enough water is tiredness or fatigue. The next symptom is often a dull headache, followed later by hunger. It's only at this stage you'll notice your thirst. Thirst is a poorly developed sense and is not a good gauge of whether you need to drink.

Even if you 'never feel thirsty', you will need to drink water. Plain water hydrates you very effectively. If you feel you are just not a 'water person', start giving yourself some positive reminders about why you want water. Make it work for you! It offers excellent assistance with appetite control.

Ask anyone how much water they should have and the usual reply will be 'eight glasses a day'. But water requirements vary, depending on individual body size and level of activity, as well as the season and environmental temperature. During the summer, 1.5 litres (six glasses) of water per day would be the least you should drink; in winter 1litre (four glasses) would be your minimum. Even if you think your water intake is fine, measure it over a couple of days to check.

It's all very well knowing how much water you should be having, but actually drinking it is another matter. Ideally, drink half your water over the morning and half over the afternoon. It's helpful to use lunchtime as a halfway check point.

A 750ml water bottle is a useful measure with which to establish your pattern: one bottle by lunch and one in the afternoon. The 750ml bottle is the equivalent of three standard glasses. Alternatively, link your water intake to mealtimes; for example, a glass with each meal, and one after each meal. Water may be taken hot or cold; it makes no difference. Work towards developing a system that comfortably fits both your weekday and your weekend lifestyle. It is a good practice to always drink water after exercise. This is in addition to your daily requirement. As time goes on, whether you are at home or travelling, working or on holiday, you want a sustainable routine to help with appetite control.

If you're not a good water drinker, build up gradually. Start with one bottle or three glasses per day. Do this for 2 – 3 weeks, gradually increasing it by another glass until you are having a minimum of 1.5 litres. Over-drinking won't do you any good. It just results in additional trips to the toilet and, possibly, a loss of water-soluble vitamins.

Is there a water that is better than others? You could have water from the tap, filtered water or purchased bottled water – whichever suits you. You need to feel good with your source of water. If you are happy with tap water – fine! Keeping your water in the fridge overnight may improve the flavour for you; so does adding sliced cucumber, lemon, strawberry, orange or fresh mint.

If you prefer bottled water, put water bottles on your weekly shopping list so

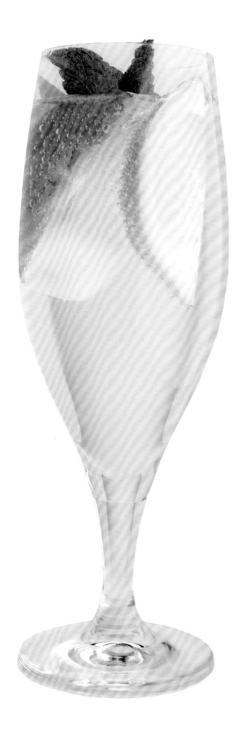

they arrive regularly and remind you to check your intake. If you're refilling plastic bottles, replace them each week, as they aren't made to be recycled long term.

Like it hot?

Tea and coffee are both free of kilojoules; however, they are also a diuretic, which means they do the opposite of hydrating your system. For weight loss, focus on an adequate water intake, and then enjoy tea and coffee in addition to that. Have milk in your hot drinks if you wish. A drink made with fat-reduced milk between meals is great, as it moves you away from looking for food, and the small amount of protein in the milk is perfect for picking you up and taking you through to your next meal.

Generally in the hot summer months 1.5 litres (six glasses) of water per day would be your minimum and in winter 1 litre (four glasses) would be your minimum. Even if you think your water intake is fine – it's worth measuring out your intake on a couple of days to check the quantities.

For variety, include other hot drinks such as hot chocolate; however, use less than the recommended quantity of powder: e.g. 1 tsp instead of 2. In a café, ask for a half-strength version.

Soups may surprise you. They are often perceived as quite suitable in a weight loss programme, but they are mainly carbohydrate and also low in fibre. A 200ml serving of many soups will provide you with kilojoules equivalent to 1 ½ slices of sandwich bread. A bowl of soup, together with a bread roll or a couple of slices of bread, can be a high-carbohydrate meal with fairly significant kilojoules. Remember that carbohydrate will only satisfy you for a couple of hours at the most before you feel hungry again. A good soup choice for weight loss would be an Asian-style soup – a clear stock with plenty of chunky green vegetables, sliced meat and some noodles – with the emphasis on more greens and not too many noodles.

What about juices and energy drinks?

Drinking your kilojoules is an easy way to gain weight, because there is no physical action of chewing which helps you feel more satisfied. The goal of weight loss is better served by chewing food (to give yourself a good sense of fullness), and drinking fluids with no or very few kilojoules (for your hydration).

Food producers would like you to believe that juices are a natural part of a healthy diet. However, even juice with no added sugar still has considerable kilojoules, because the naturally occurring fruit sugar is the same as the white sugar in your sugar bowl. Freshly squeezed juice from fruit grown in your back garden is the same as any other juice. Vegetable juices are higher in kilojoules than you would anticipate. Energy drinks sound promising – but are ideal for people who want to gain weight! Protein shakes and smoothies are full of kilojoules and are not helpful for long-term weight loss.

Alcohol

Alcohol doesn't have to be taken out of your life; it's just a matter of knowing how to include it in a way that is suitable for you while you are losing weight.

A glass of alcohol provides kilojoules from both the carbohydrate and the alcohol components. A 200ml serving of wine, or a generous nip of gin with tonic, or 400mls of beer every day for a year, provides the kilojoules to add 9kgs to your weight over that time. However, the biggest impact of alcohol is that it reduces your blood sugar levels and, over the following 24 hours after drinking, you will be hungrier. It is probably the best appetite stimulant you could take! You may notice if you have a 'big' night out that either later that evening, or the next day, you will be hungrier than usual. If you drink on a daily basis you probably won't notice this increased appetite, but it will be there.

Unfortunately, no one alcoholic drink is better than any other for weight loss. All

This = that
fluid portions

Fruit juice 190mls

Chocolate milk 165mls

Ginger ale 190mls

Tonic water 190mls

Soft drink 125mls

Vegetable juice 165mls

Tomato juice 250mls

Milk – dark blue 125mls

Milk – trim 190mls

Energy drink 125mls

These fluids are all in portions of a similar kilojoule value, and for simplicity can be described as 1 UNIT.

of them stimulate an appetite. 'Lite' and low carb beers have fewer calories, but the difference is not as much as you would hope. It does all come down to volume consumed!

After a week of increased socialising, it is helpful to tighten your intake the following week. Yes, it's always easy to put extra in and difficult to find a suitable time to take some out.

For many, alcohol is a part of daily life, but it is well worth aiming for more alcohol-free days. Consider keeping alcohol for weekends and special occasions, rather than for everyday use. Abstaining from alcohol all together for a couple of months isn't that helpful, as the problem returns when the alcohol is reintroduced.

The encouraging side is that, as you lose weight, your capacity for alcohol – and often even your desire for it – will reduce.

Suitable options

Water is the best fluid for you, but sometimes you may want a different flavour. Sparkling water with a dash of lime juice or low-kilojoule cordial are both suitable options. Soda water has no kilojoules and if it is from your soda stream it is just aerated water, so it can replace your regular water. Soda from a bottle has a higher level of sodium so will not help with hydration. However, you can use it as an option on

"How much Sugar is in your Drinks?"

Soft drink 250ml glass **5 ½ teaspoons**	**Powdered drink** 250ml glass **6 teaspoons**
Energy drink 250ml glass **9 teaspoons**	**Fruit juice no added sugar** 250ml glass **6 teaspoons**
Sports drink 250ml glass **4 teaspoons**	**Flavoured milk** 250ml box **6 ½ teaspoons**

your alcohol-free nights, maybe with a splash of bitters, lemon or lime – and make it glamorous with ice and a slice in a tall glass!

Artificially sweetened drinks contain no kilojoules. These drinks are certainly a suitable option for someone who enjoys sweet drinks, but should be taken in addition to water rather than as a replacement for it. Once your weight is down and you are maintaining an active lifestyle with a good water intake, you could then move to the occasional drink sweetened with sugar rather than an artificial sweetener.

Clear soups such as miso, or soups made from stock with only 'unrestricted' vegetables added, are good warming drinks in the winter. They contain very few kilojoules and may be taken with meals, or between meals. If you are using commercially prepared stocks, choose low-salt products, otherwise you will become too thirsty.

> A hungry person may, in fact, just be a thirsty person.

This = that
alcohol portions

White wine 100ml

Red wine 100ml

Beer 200ml

Lite beer 300ml

Gin & tonic 120mls

Brandy 40mls

These drinks are all in portions of a similar kilojoule value, and for simplicity can be described as 1 UNIT.

This = that fluid units

The following fluids are all in portions of a similar kilojoule value, and for simplicity can be described as 1 UNIT. For example 200mls of standard beer is 1 UNIT and has similar kilojoules to 100mls of wine, which is also 1 UNIT. In other words this = that as every item on the list is 1 UNIT.

Type of Alcohol	Serving Size
Beer – standard (draught/lager)	200 mls
Beer – stout	250 mls
Lite beer	250 mls
Wine – white/red	100 mls
Sparkling	100 mls
Sherry – medium	60 mls
Spirits	40mls

Fluids (1 glass = 250 mls)	Serving Size
Fruit juice	¾ glass
Carrot juice	1 glass
Tomato juice	1 glass
Vegetable juice	⅔ glass
Tonic water	¾ glass
Soft drinks e.g. lemonade/coke	½ glass
Energy drink	½ glass
Powerade	1 glass
Mizone	2 glasses
Lime cordial concentrate	4 tbsp
Sweet drink powder	1 tbsp
Complan	2 tbsp
Milo powder	2 ½ tbsp
Nesquik powder	3 tbsp
Ovaltine	3 tbsp
Pumpkin soup (homemade)	⅔ cup
Packet of cup of soup	⅔ packet

7

Stepping out

Change the emphasis
Enjoy the support
Born to walk
Pamper yourself

Change the emphasis

For some reason, exercise is often the first subject people want to discuss when talking about the changes they are making for weight loss. You may have seen for yourself that even when you include regular exercise such as sessions at the gym, workouts with personal trainers, pilates and yoga classes, swimming, daily dog walking, running, golf and tennis, it doesn't shed weight as you feel it should. You can work out and exercise on a very regular basis – yes, spend plenty of precious time getting hot and sweaty, day after day – with very disappointing weight loss results – if any. It may seem cruel but how much you sweat is no indication of how effective the exercise is.

Go back to the basic equation for weight loss, where energy intake needs to be less than energy output. In other words, eat less, and exercise more. It looks simple on paper but getting the balance right is not as straightforward as it sounds.

When you have a higher body fat, exercise becomes less effective in reducing your weight. You can put a lot of time into physical activity but the kilojoules it uses are negligible. With the technology to measure body makeup, you can see for yourself that when you carry extra body fat, increasing your exercise can make very little difference to the numbers.

If you have a high body fat along with a high level of muscle, exercise for longer than 35 minutes may just make you a hungrier person over the following 24 hours.

The balance for weight loss is certainly tilted to what you eat rather than how much you exercise.

Enjoy the support

But don't be put off exercise as there are good reasons that it appears vital to the weight loss equation. Exercise keeps your attitude positive and your mind more focused. When you exercise regularly, it helps with control and you'll be more inclined to identify portions that are suitable for you, and more likely to change your old food patterns and choices.

There may be all sorts of reasons you find exercise difficult and it's easy not to find the time. But don't look for the excuses why not to exercise; look for the reasons why you should. Once you start regular exercise, you'll find it gives you more energy. Yes, using energy creates more energy.

Exercise offers you great support, so bring it in and make it work for you.

Born to walk

There's lots of marketing out there for weight loss exercise – gyms, pools, fitness classes, various types of equipment – all promising you magnificent success. But the most effective and probably the cheapest exercise is walking. You were born to walk and it's excellent for what you want to do with your weight.

> Exercise doesn't need to be set up as a chore – turn it into a time to pamper yourself!

Keep your walks short, brisk and daily. Half an hour is perfect; any longer than 35 minutes may just make you hungry. Even 15 minutes a day is not a waste of time. The pace is important; stride out on the flat and push yourself along. At the end, you want to feel you couldn't have covered more distance in that time. Generally, a walking speed of 3.5kms in 30 minutes is effective, but be realistic with your expectations of yourself. Maybe you will need to build up to this speed gradually. If you want to walk for more than 30 minutes, you could split it up with 30 minutes in the morning and 15 – 30 minutes in the afternoon, so you don't get too hungry. When you carry extra weight, walking is kinder to your joints than running. Save that for when you have lost weight.

By all means keep up your gym sessions or

> Exercise for longer than 35 minutes may just make you a hungrier person over the following 24 hours.

fitness classes, but for weight loss put your emphasis on a short brisk walk every day. Any other fitness is an 'extra' on top of that. Once you have your body fat near the normal range, then sessions at the gym will be more effective at increasing muscle mass.

Pamper yourself

The success of exercise depends on having it scheduled into your day as if it were an appointment. The 30 minutes needs an allocated time slot set in concrete! It doesn't matter what time of the day you take your walk, but the earlier in the day you do it, the less likely it is to get lost. Aim to make it part of your morning routine – as natural an act as putting your shirt on before you leave the house. Others may find lunchtime works for them. If you are walking at the end of the day, it may be helpful to see it as part of the work day and walk before you arrive home.

Some people will have a summer and a winter routine. Summer lends itself to morning walks and as the days shorten you may need to alter this routine – perhaps even consider hiring a treadmill for the winter months.

Exercise will only be beneficial when you are feeling well. If you do get sick, stop walking, recover, and then get back into it.

There will be times when your routine is upset and the exercise drops out. Success with long-term weight control depends on being able to pick it up again when the timing is right; by adjusting your routine, establishing the time slot and getting going again.

A step counter is a helpful tool for seeing how much you move over the course of a day. You may well feel you are on the go most of the time, however the step counter will give you an actual measure. Put it on for the whole day. If it clocks more than 12,000 steps per day – great. If you are doing less than 8,000 steps per day, you'll need to set goals to gradually increase this. Every 10 minutes of walking adds an extra 1000 steps.

Exercise doesn't need to be set up as a chore – turn it into a time to pamper yourself! Maybe you could start out walking just in the weekends and then move it into the week – even if it is just a 15-minute walk on some days. Wrap your arms around your exercise time and see it as a pleasure. The beauty of walking is you can do it anywhere, anytime and, apart from a good pair of shoes, no special equipment is required. It's also good for heart health, good for mobility, good for stress levels and good for your soul.

> You need to walk the dog every day, even if you don't have a dog!

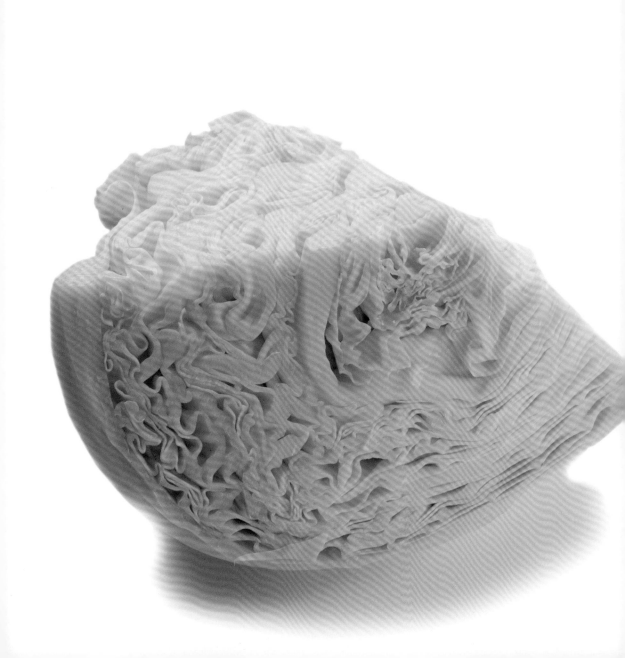

8

Putting it all together

Create your framework
Design your meals
Work on routines
Shop with permission

Create your framework

This is the exciting part. You can now work on your own framework of food, fluid and exercise, and start filling in the blanks.

First, use your body composition monitor to find out how much muscle and how much fat you have. The monitor will also provide a basal or resting metabolic rate and that is the number you are interested in. To keep this part simple, we have provided four base plans. Choose the one that fits with your metabolic rate (see pages 74-77) .

These plans are suggested daily intakes. We've put in the food choices for your meals and included the fluids and exercise. However, you can adjust your plan by referring to the Unit lists in the various chapters (carbohydrates page 34, proteins page 44, fats page 53, fluids and alcohol page 63). For example, you may not be interested in alcohol so this unit could be replaced with more carbohydrate or protein. The Unit lists will make it possible to enjoy plenty of variety. It's simply a matter of making it work for you.

Design your meals

Knowing your body makeup will give you direction on how to put your meals together.

Breakfast: This meal will set you up well for the rest of the day. The higher your muscle mass and metabolic rate, the more important protein is at your breakfast. Adding 'unrestricted' vegetables, such as tomatoes, mushrooms and spinach leaves, offers extra fibre to keep you feeling fuller for longer. Breakfast usually wants to be quick, functional, and of course, delicious. Often it's just a matter of rotating 3 or 4 favourite selections over the week. Make sure you have enough variety and, typically, 6 eggs per week would be the maximum.

Mid-morning: Once you are in the pattern of a good breakfast, the mid-morning snack becomes less important. A milky drink fits in well here, as it provides you with carbohydrate and protein while moving you away from looking for food.

Lunch: There are 3 items you'll be looking for when choosing your lunch. First, you'll want a good portion of 'unrestricted' vegetables. These could be salad, stir fried or cooked vegetables. Frozen greens can offer a good backup. Then include some protein, such as meat, chicken, fish or a vegetarian option, and then a carbohydrate, which could be a bread product, rice, pasta, or a starchy vegetable. Experiment until you find suitable lunch options for your needs and tastes. You may have a pattern of taking lunch with you, or if you prefer to buy, it may be a matter of finding a couple of lunch bars or cafes that provide choices to fit your requirements.

Mid-afternoon: A snack in the afternoon is important, not necessarily because you are hungry by this point, but to help with appetite control for the evening meal. This is especially true if you have a high muscle mass. Dairy items (such as yoghurt) and fruit provide a functional and portion-controlled snack. The dairy is helpful again for its 'snack-sized' protein, and the chewing of fruit will help with appetite satisfaction.

The evening meal: For most people this is the main meal of the day, and should contain four particular components. The first is plenty of 'unrestricted' vegetables – whether they are hot, cold, cooked or raw makes no difference. Chapter 13 has simple, tasty recipe suggestions. Ideally these vegetables should cover half the plate as they effectively provide no kilojoules. You also want two starchy carbohydrates in different colours, such as yellow, orange, and white; e.g. pumpkin, kumara, corn, beetroot, potato, rice, pasta and noodles. Lastly, add the protein, such as meat, poultry, fish, eggs or a vegetarian option. Aim to eat fish twice a week, and red meat twice a week for the iron it provides. The remainder of the protein meals could be chicken, eggs or a vegetarian protein.

Supper: Altering your food intake over the day and changing the types of food you are choosing at meals will reduce your need to eat in the evening. Depending on how you distribute your specified portions over the day, you may have a fruit platter or a hot milky drink.

Adding plenty of unrestricted vegetables to this meal has virtually halved the number of kilojoules.

Metabolic Rate Under 6000KJ (1400kcals)

DAILY UNITS: 6 Carbohydrate Units (3 breads/cereals, 2 starchy vegetable, 1 fruit)
               6 Protein Units (include 2 dairy units)
               1 Oil/Fat Unit e.g. spreads for breads and in cooking
               ½ Alcohol Unit
               = 13 ½ TOTAL DAILY UNITS

DAILY WATER: 2 x 750ml bottles = 6 glasses (½ in morning and ½ in afternoon)

OTHER FLUIDS: Hot fluids, plus water after exercise

ALCOHOL: 3 – 4 x 120ml glasses per week

DAILY EXERCISE: 30 minutes very brisk walking. Time: 6.30am or 5pm

SUGGESTED DAILY MEAL PLAN

UNIT LAYOUT	MEAL PLAN
BREAKFAST: 7.30am – 8.00am	
2 Carbohydrate Units	*2 Breads–brown/grain–thin butter/table spread*
1 Protein Unit	*1 egg or ⅓ cup baked beans or ½ cup cottage cheese*
Plus unrestricted vegetables	*Plenty of tomatoes/spinach/mushrooms*
MID-MORNING: 10.30AM – 11.00AM	*Tea or coffee*
LUNCH: Approx 12.30pm	
1 Carbohydrate Unit	*1 Bread or 2 ryvita crackers–thin butter/table spread*
1 Protein Unit	*50g ham or 1 chicken drumstick*
Plus unrestricted vegetables	*Plenty of unrestricted vegetables e.g. salad, stir fry vegetables – aim at 2 cups*
MID-AFTERNOON: 3.30pm-4.00pm	
1 Carbohydrate Unit	*1 Fruit – get variety*
2 Protein Units (dairy)	*1 pot of yoghurt (150g)*
EVENING MEAL: 6.30pm	
2 Carbohydrate Units	
2 Protein Units	
Plus ½ plate unrestricted vegetables	
SUPPER:	*Fluid only or maybe fruit from afternoon*

½ cup potato
½ cup kumara
¼ single chicken breast
Plenty of unrestricted vegetables/ salad (generous ½ plate)

Metabolic Rate 6000-7000KJ (1400-1650kcals)

DAILY UNITS:	7 Carbohydrate Units (4 breads/cereals, 2 starchy vegetable, 1 fruit)
	7 Protein Units (include 3 dairy units)
	1 Oil/Fat Unit e.g. spreads for breads and in cooking
	½ Alcohol Unit
	= 15 ½ TOTAL DAILY UNITS

DAILY WATER: 2 x 750ml bottles = 6 glasses (½ in morning and ½ in afternoon)

OTHER FLUIDS: Hot fluids, plus water after exercise

ALCOHOL: 3 – 4 x 120ml glasses per week

DAILY EXERCISE: 30 minutes very brisk walking. Time: 6.30am or 5pm

SUGGESTED DAILY MEAL PLAN

UNIT LAYOUT	MEAL PLAN
BREAKFAST: 7.30am – 8.00am	
2 Carbohydrate Units	*2 Breads–brown/grain–thin butter/table spread*
1 Protein Unit	*1 egg or ⅓ cup baked beans or ½ cup cottage cheese*
Plus unrestricted vegetables	*Plenty of tomatoes/spinach/mushrooms*
MID-MORNING: 10.30AM – 11.00AM	
1 Protein Unit (dairy)	*Small trim flat white*
LUNCH: Approx 12.30pm	
2 Carbohydrate Unit	*2 Breads–thin butter/table spread*
1 Protein Unit	*50g ham or 50g chicken or ½ tin sardines*
Plus unrestricted vegetables	*Plenty of unrestricted vegetables e.g. salad, stir fry vegetables – aim at 2 cups*
MID-AFTERNOON: 3.30pm-4.00pm	
1 Carbohydrate Unit	*1 Fruit – get variety*
2 Protein Units (dairy)	*1 pot of yoghurt (150g)*
EVENING MEAL: 6.30pm	
2 Carbohydrate Units	
2 Protein Units	
Plus ½ plate unrestricted vegetables	
SUPPER:	*Fluid only or maybe fruit from afternoon*

Evening meal pie chart:
- ½ cup white rice
- ½ cup corn
- Small steak (100g)
- Plenty of unrestricted vegetables/salad (generous ½ plate)

Metabolic Rate 7000-8000KJ (1650-1900kcals)

DAILY UNITS:	8 Carbohydrate Units (4 breads/cereals, 2 starchy vegetable, 2 fruit)
	8 Protein Units (include 3 dairy units)
	2 Oil/Fat Units e.g. spreads for breads and in cooking
	1 Alcohol Unit
	= 19 TOTAL DAILY UNITS

DAILY WATER: 2 x 750ml bottles = 6 glasses (½ in morning and ½ in afternoon)

OTHER FLUIDS: Hot fluids, plus water after exercise

ALCOHOL: 7 x 120ml glasses per week

DAILY EXERCISE: 30 minutes very brisk walking. Time: 6.30am or 5pm

SUGGESTED DAILY MEAL PLAN

UNIT LAYOUT	MEAL PLAN
BREAKFAST: 7.30am – 8.00am	
2 Carbohydrate Units	*2 Breads–thin butter/table spread*
2 Protein Unit	*2 eggs or ⅔ cup baked beans or ⅔ cup savoury mince*
Plus unrestricted vegetables	*Plenty of tomatoes/spinach/mushrooms*
MID-MORNING: 10.30AM – 11.00AM	
1 Protein Unit (dairy)	*Small trim latté*
LUNCH: Approx 12.30pm	
2 Carbohydrate Units	*2 Bread or 4 ryvita crackers–thin butter/table spread*
1 Protein Unit	*50g ham or 50g chicken or 75g tinned tuna*
Plus unrestricted vegetables	*Plenty of unrestricted vegetables e.g. salad, stir fry vegetables – aim at 2 cups*
MID-AFTERNOON: 3.30pm-4.00pm	
1 Carbohydrate Unit	*1 Fruit – get variety*
2 Protein Units (dairy)	*1 pot of yoghurt (150g)*
EVENING MEAL: 6.30pm	
2 Carbohydrate Units	
2 Protein Units	
Plus ½ plate unrestricted vegetables	
SUPPER: 8.30PM	
1 Carbohydrate Unit	*1 Fruit*

Metabolic Rate Over 8000KJ (1900kcals)

DAILY UNITS: 9 Carbohydrate Units (5 breads/cereals, 2 starchy vegetable, 2 fruit)
9 Protein Units (include 4 dairy units)
2 Oil/Fat Units e.g. spreads for breads and in cooking
1 Alcohol Unit
= 21 TOTAL DAILY UNITS

DAILY WATER: 2 x 750ml bottles = 6 glasses (½ in morning and ½ in afternoon)

OTHER FLUIDS: Hot fluids, plus water after exercise

ALCOHOL: 7 x 120ml glasses per week

DAILY EXERCISE: 30 minutes very brisk walking. Time: 6.30am or 5pm

SUGGESTED DAILY MEAL PLAN

UNIT LAYOUT	MEAL PLAN
BREAKFAST: 7.30am – 8.00am	
2 Carbohydrate Units	*2 Breads–thin butter/table spread*
2 Protein Units	*2 eggs or ⅔ cup baked beans or ⅔ cup savoury mince*
Plus unrestricted vegetables	*Plenty of tomatoes/spinach/mushrooms*
MID-MORNING: 10.30AM – 11.00AM	
2 Protein Units (dairy)	*Large trim latté*
LUNCH: Approx 12.30pm	
3 Carbohydrate Unit	*3 Breads or 1 ½ cups rice or 1 large bread roll*
1 Protein Unit	*50g ham or 50g chicken or 70g tinned salmon*
Plus unrestricted vegetables	*Plenty of unrestricted vegetables e.g. salad, stir fry vegetables – aim at 2 cups*
MID-AFTERNOON: 3.30pm-4.00pm	
1 Carbohydrate Unit	*1 Fruit – get variety*
2 Protein Units (dairy)	*1 pot of yoghurt (150g)*
EVENING MEAL: 6.30pm	
2 Carbohydrate Units	
2 Protein Units	
Plus ½ plate unrestricted vegetables	
SUPPER: 8.30PM	
1 Carbohydrate Unit	*1 Fruit*

For the evening meal section:

½ cup potato
½ cup corn
⅔ cup of mince
Plenty of unrestricted vegetables/salad (generous ½ plate)

Develop sustainable routines: three meals evenly distributed over the day, a system for your water intake, and a time for your daily exercise.

Work on routines

Establishing routines is important for weight control. Behind routines there is organisation and planning, which are key words in successful long-term weight management. Develop sustainable routines; three meals evenly distributed over the day, a system for your water intake and a time for your daily exercise. You want strong routines that will remain intact today, tomorrow, two months down the track, and two years – and more – from now. Challenges will affect your routines; for instance, sickness, houseguests, holidays, projects with deadlines, stressful periods and different shifts at work, to name a few. The way to cope with these difficult times is to draw a line at some stage, knowing that by that point you will be able to get yourself back onto your base routine. As you lose weight and gain energy, you will see the benefit these routines offer and they will become easier and easier to work with. In fact, they will become your normal pattern.

Dividing your daily food into a 3-meal structure rather than grazing over the day, results in more successful weight loss. With the emphasis on three good meals per day this simple structure allows you to easily keep tabs on your intake. Ideally you want to develop a firm pattern for your meal times, with breakfast between 7.30 – 8.30am, lunch between 12.00 – 1.30pm, and the evening meal by 7.00 – 7.30pm at the latest. Breakfast will fuel you sufficiently to get you through to lunch, maybe with a small 'top up' mid-morning. Refuelling at lunch will take you through to the evening meal, especially when you 'top up' in the afternoon, not because you are necessarily hungry at that time, but to make sure you are not too hungry when you sit down for the evening meal. If, however, you are a shift worker, you will need to create a structure that suits your circumstances. Some planning will be required, especially if your shifts vary. If you consistently work a late or early shift, then schedule all three meals later or earlier in the day. It's a little more challenging when the shifts vary, though. The best option is to 'anchor' your breakfast somewhere between 6.30 and 9.30am, and the evening meal 12 hours later. Lunch then becomes a meal at either midday or midnight, depending on the shift.

Shop with permission

Support your food choices with a good shopping routine so you have easy access to your food. Shop on a weekly basis and, if you need to, pick up more 'unrestricted' vegetables mid-week. Familiarity with your supermarket layout will make it easier and quicker. Find a day and a time in the day that works for you – but don't shop when you are hungry, or all sorts of unnecessary extras will drop into that trolley!

Make a point of buying only what is on your shopping list, in suitable portion sizes. Be careful with the treats for visitors or other family members, as they will be hard to resist. However as you lose weight this control will improve.

Use the shopping list (page 81) as a guide, and modify it to suit your needs and your supermarket layout.

> Support your food choices with a good shopping routine so you have easy access to your food.

A good shopping list will put a lot of your menu planning in place. Ideally, it will follow the flow of your supermarket so you don't have to back track. Generally speaking, the outside aisles of the supermarket will be where you need to spend your time. That's where you'll find the fresh, unprocessed products, such as fruit and vegetables, meat, poultry, fish, and breads. The centre aisles are stocked with the more processed products, with high fats and sugars which are sometimes hard to identify. You don't need to spend much time in these centre aisles at all.

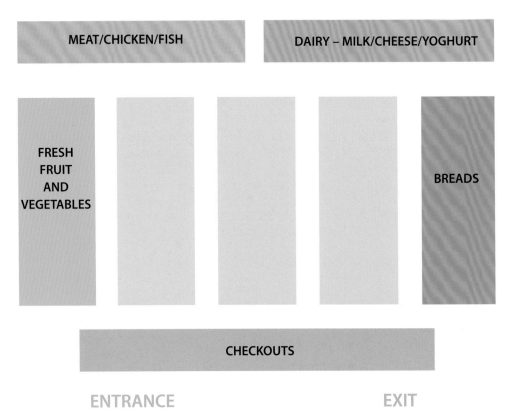

SUPERMARKET LAYOUT

MEAT/CHICKEN/FISH	DAIRY – MILK/CHEESE/YOGHURT

FRESH FRUIT AND VEGETABLES

BREADS

CHECKOUTS

ENTRANCE   EXIT

WEEKLY SHOPPING LIST

Item	Quantity	Item	Quantity
Vegetables		Jam	
greens		Honey	
salad items		Spreads	
orange/yellow		Vegemite	
Potatoes		Pickled vegetables	
Fresh herbs		Oil	
Fruit		Vinegar	
Meat		Balsamic vinegar	
Chicken		Dressings	
Fish/seafood		Tomato Sauce	
Cold cuts		Soy sauce	
Smoked chicken		Thai chilli sauce	
Bacon		Worcestershire sauce	
Eggs		Salt and pepper	
Cheese		Stock	
Milk		Tea/coffee/Milo	
Yoghurt		Wine/beer and mixers	
Butter/table spread		Bottled water	
Breads		Gladwrap	
Pita breads/bread rolls		Foil	
Breakfast cereal		Baking paper	
Tinned vegetables		Paper towels	
Baked beans		Serviettes	
Tinned fish		Laundry items	
Tinned fruit/pots of fruit		Cleaning agents	
Rice – white/brown		Bathroom/toilet items	
Pasta		Personal items	
Couscous		Fly spray	
Noodles		Batteries	
Tinned soups/soup mix			
Crackers			

Portions, portions, portions

You can eat everything
The right size for your size
Tips for control
Eating out

You can eat everything

Eventually you want to be able to eat everything – and you will, once you get to grips with identifying how much and how often is suitable for you. You'll even be able to manage foods higher in fats and sugars – if the portions are the right size. That's why weight loss is not about insisting that you eat only 'healthily'. It's about you seeing all foods in suitable portion sizes, then being able to tell yourself 'Thanks, that's enough, kindly stop eating!'

As soon as your weight increases by even just 3 – 4 kgs, your appetite also increases and from there, it's easy to overeat. You are working to 'reset' the present portion picture you have for yourself. The lists and pictures in the various chapters are to help you visualise portion sizes of similar kilojoule value, and to guide you when making choices on your personalised food plan. You won't need to use these lists forever as, with time, you will know automatically what size portion suits you.

> Instead of seeing portions as smaller than you would like, see them as 'perfect for the new you'.

The right size for your size

Give yourself positive messages about how much you are eating. Instead of seeing portions as smaller than you would like, see them as 'perfect for the new you'. It's about feeding a smaller person, and making sure the portions fit. In the past as you gained weight you were selecting portions for the wrong sized person. With plenty of access to food and drinks, it's all too easy to do that and then the habit of slightly larger portions is reinforced as your appetite increases. It is now time to change that pattern and to start feeding the smaller person. See the changes as a way of pampering yourself with perfect portions. Yes, they are perfect for you and it is all about you! The right portion size will get easier and easier to choose as you lose weight.

Eating out

It's perfectly possible to eat out, enjoy yourself, and still control your weight. Whether it's for breakfast, lunch or dinner, keep referring to your usual requirements; plenty of greens, care with portion sizes and low in fats and oils.

Breakfast: You're in luck if you like eggs, because they're always on the menu, along with tomatoes and mushrooms; so it's just a matter of asking for a suitable portion size. Other protein options that may be available are baked beans, old fashioned savoury mince, lean ham or bacon, breakfast sausages and maybe fish in some form such as fish cakes. Steer away from high-carb, high-fat

Tips for control

If you do feel hungry, check the following 10 tips are in place for good appetite control:

- Drink enough water – a thirsty person is a hungry person.
- Eat plenty of greens at lunch and dinner, as they will keep the portions in the rest of the meal smaller.
- Choose food, not fluids – chewing your food at meals helps you feel fuller, rather than meals you drink, such as soups or smoothies.
- Early to bed! A tired person is a hungry person.
- Minimum of three meals each day. Studies show that when you miss a meal, you'll eat more than those missing kilojoules in addition to your normal intake over the next 24 hours.
- 'You are when you eat'. Long gaps between meals just promote overeating. Regular meal and snack times will help keep your blood sugar levels stable and this improves appetite control.
- Use a smaller plate for your evening meal – simple, but very effective.
- Buy less, cook less and eat less – it makes getting the perfect portion easier.
- Reduce your alcohol intake – alcohol drives down your blood sugar levels, causing you to feel hungry.
- Keep your 'small and delicious' motto close by when choosing your food.

choices such as streaky bacon and hash browns, or even the healthy-sounding toasted muesli with fruit and yoghurt.

Lunch: In some ways lunch may be the most difficult meal when eating out.

Look for carbohydrate – which is usually readily available and typically would be bread, rice, potato or pasta – but check that you are not being served an overly large portion. You want some protein, too, such as meat, chicken, fish or a vegetarian option. Lastly, you do want a large, leafy seasonal salad or a bowl of steaming vegetables to give you fibre and fullness for the afternoon, but this last component is frequently not easy to find, or the portion is small.

With time you'll get to know places where the food selection or menu is perfect for your needs.

Evening meal: It's usually easy to control what time you eat at home, but when you are out it may be a couple of hours later. This time delay sets you up to be hungrier when you are working with smaller portions and it could be easy to overeat both on nibbles and the meal by the time it does arrive. A plate of 'unrestricted' vegetables before you head out the door will give you improved control in this situation. This could simply be sliced tomato, cucumber and basil with a good dressing, or a handful of frozen green beans, microwaved and topped with sweet chilli and soy sauce.

It's perfectly possible to eat out, enjoy yourself, and still control your weight.

Once out, do your best to get the right-sized meal in front of you – it's too easy to overeat if the serving is too large. Keep the emphasis on plenty of greens: volunteer to bring a salad if going to a friend's house or always ask for sides of 'unrestricted' vegetables when ordering off a menu. The occasional dessert – preferably shared, if you're with a compliant dinner companion – is not a problem.

Pace yourself with alcohol as it turns you into a hungrier person. It's a good policy to follow each glass of alcohol with at least one glass of water.

While eating out may be challenging, it's also fun, usually very pleasurable and you want a life while you lose weight. So do the best you can, and put yourself back on track again the following day with your food choices and portions.

It's a good policy to follow each glass of alcohol with at least one glass of water.

10

Live your dream!

Take control
Getting smaller
Keep a record
Predict success
Living in a fat world

Take control

Plotting a path for your weight is similar to creating an itinerary for a trip. Think about how you organise your holidays. You decide on your destination and how much time you've got to work with. You plan where you will go each day, calculating what is a reasonable distance to cover. The longer the journey, the more planning you need to do, because you want to have a fabulous time.

You can now apply this system to your weight. Decide where you want to go, and set up a time frame for reaching your goal. Break the weight loss process into stages, 5 or 10kgs at a time. Make notes for yourself; map out the different stages and the time involved. Be realistic, and remember you want to enjoy a normal life while you lose weight, or you will be heading – once again – down that 'no win' diet track. You want the freedom to accept the dinner invitations, enjoy your food, live your usual life with

> If you do it right, you'll only have to do it once and you'll enjoy the control and success forever.

family and friends, keep great health and have good energy levels.

The rate of weight loss will not be the same for everyone. An acceptable goal is 2kgs a month. It may not sound a lot, but it's 24kgs in a year – and that's a great result. Weight seems to just drop off some people and they comfortably lose a kilogram per week. Others are quite happy with a consistent kilogram a month. These are all significant weight losses over a year – especially when it is forever! Success of diets has often been measured by how fast weight is lost. However you need to see the true success of weight loss is in establishing patterns so that every kilo lost is lost for good.

> Success of diets has often been measured by how fast weight is lost. However you need to see the true success of weight loss is in establishing patterns so that every kilo lost is lost for good.

Getting smaller

Keep checking your relationship with 'The Big Three' – food, fluid and exercise. Weighing yourself every 1 or 2 weeks will tell you if you have the balance right. Remember, you have a history of taking a few inconspicuous extras, and those patterns are strong. Every time you lose a kilogram of body fat, remind yourself you are feeding a smaller person, keep adjusting your portions, and push the pace of your walking.

Predict success

The following factors have regularly been shown to predict how successful your weight loss will be.

- A focus on health. For individuals with health issues such as raised cholesterol, raised blood sugars, raised blood pressure or arthritis in lower body joints, the health benefits of weight loss have been shown to be strong motivating factors.
- The number of previous attempts to lose weight. If you have a history of unsuccessful diet attempts, it's time to move away from the 'diet mode' and look ahead to permanent, sustainable lifestyle changes.
- A sense of personal responsibility. It is important to believe you can lose weight and to have a strong intention of making changes.
- Realistic goals. A goal of 5 – 10kg at a time is ideal. The goal can be reset each time one has been achieved.
- A written record. Keeping notes of everything you eat and drink and how active you are is invaluable.

Keep a record

Recording your food and fluid intake along with your daily exercise is crucial. Take two minutes at the end of each day and write down everything in a food diary. Be specific with your portions. If you had extras somewhere in the day or an over-sized meal, note it down, along with how you compensated by reducing portions later on (see form page 92).

Learn where your boundaries are. By checking meal times, alcohol, water and exercise, you will identify your hunger trends and be able to tweak your plan accordingly. You'll probably need to keep records for at least the first month.

Living in a fat world

Unfortunately, it's true – you are living in a fat world and the statistics are only getting worse. The World Health Organisation describes obesity as a modern problem. It's hard to believe, but statistics for overweight and obesity did not exist 50 years ago, because it wasn't an issue. Going by the present trends, even those presently without weight issues will find it increasingly difficult to maintain their situation. So dig your toes in and be determined. If you do it right, you'll only have to do it once and you'll enjoy the control and success forever.

Record the intake of all foods and fluids – note portions and cooking techniques

BREAKFAST	MID AM	LUNCH	MID PM
DAY: _____			
Time:	Time:	Time:	Time:
DAY: _____			
Time:	Time:	Time:	Time:
DAY: _____			
Time:	Time:	Time:	Time:
DAY: _____			
Time:	Time:	Time:	Time:

EVENING MEAL	SUPPER		
		Exercise type	
		Time taken	
		Steps	
		Water	
Time:	Time:	Alcohol	
		Exercise type	
		Time taken	
		Steps	
		Water	
Time:	Time:	Alcohol	
		Exercise type	
		Time taken	
		Steps	
		Water	
Time:	Time:	Alcohol	
		Exercise type	
		Time taken	
		Steps	
		Water	
Time:	Time:	Alcohol	

11

Make it delicious

Getting good food fast
Refuse the bland and boring
Take a take-away
Stocking the pantry

Getting good food fast

Time is often one of the biggest hurdles to putting a suitable and delicious evening meal on the table. Projects and deadlines make working hours longer, travelling time is often a factor, and after-school activities means performing a juggling act between being driver, chef and homework helper. Also, spending time in the kitchen whipping up a treat is not everyone's idea of a fabulous end to the day.

On the other hand, great tasting food will allow you to walk away from the table enjoying a delicious sense of contentment. Quick, slap-together meals that are low in flavour are often followed by a hunger for something else to eat – something tasty, which usually means high in sugar and fat. However, a little organisation can make a big difference. For easy access to the right foods, do a regular weekly shop. If the shopping falls over, it'll be the 'unrestricted vegetables' that don't make it to the plate – and that's not good enough for you, is it? Guard your shopping time fiercely or, if need be, consider doing it online.

It's difficult to pull together the right sort of dinner when you arrive home late with no idea of what to have. Clearing away after the evening meal is a good time to plan dinner for the following night. Take the meat or chicken out of the freezer if necessary, and decide on the vegetables. There may be one or two evenings when you cook enough for two meals, so you don't have to start from the beginning the next night. For example, a roast meal one night is great for cold cuts the next night. Mince is very versatile and can be turned into a cottage pie, or spiced up a little and kidney beans added to make burritos or chilli con carne. Casseroles are even more delicious the next day.

In preparation for busy times you may want to do some freezer cooking in the weekend. Even a double batch made every second weekend will allow you to accumulate a selection of frozen meals. This is a time-consuming part of the meal all organised, leaving you with just the vegetables to prepare in the evening.

Refuse the bland and boring

Years ago, weight loss was a sentence to meals grilled, steamed or poached, and, if there was any sauce at all, it would be thin and tasteless. How miserable was that? You need to look on those days of diets and bland, boring food as history. You're living in a time where putting flavours into food without adding lots of kilojoules is easy, thanks to the readily available selection of sauces, spices and herbs, both locally produced and imported, in your supermarket. The problem is that fats and oils add flavour to your food very easily and many currently popular cooking styles do involve using fats and oils. However, you don't need to use special low-kilojoule recipe books. With your new awareness of hidden kilojoules, take any of your favourite recipes and adapt them to suit you.

But as you know, it's not just about looking for the kilojoules. Keep portion sizes in mind, too. If the family wants fish and chips, you'll eat a lot less if half your plate is covered with a fresh seasonal salad. If you were meeting

A few simple suggestions on how you can adapt your recipes:

- When putting oil into a pan, wipe the oil around with a paper towel to remove any excess.
- Be careful with cheeses. Replace a cheese topping with toasted breadcrumbs and a 'dusting' of grated cheese. The cheese in a white sauce could be replaced with finely chopped parsley and whole seed mustard – still very tasty!
- Nuts and seeds should be reduced, or could be left out all together.
- Cream and sour cream are for occasional use only. Depending on the recipe, you could use either yoghurt or cottage cheese.
- Golden brown, crispy foods such as taco shells and crispy noodles have that texture because they have been deep fried and this boosts the kilojoules fast. Taco shells could be replaced by burritos or rice, and crispy noodles could be replaced with toasted croutons or plain noodles.
- Roast vegetables and wedges can be cooked on 'fan bake' with very little oil and they will still brown well. A sprinkle of mustard powder adds to the flavour.

friends in the park for this meal you could always have the salad before you go, then you'd have better control over your portions. It's often all the little changes that give the big result.

Take a take-away

For times when you want to pick up a fast meal, there are many suitable choices available. While you're losing weight you'll be looking for dishes with low fats and oils and plenty of greens. Most fast food outlets now have salads on the menu, wraps that will be packed full of greens, and options that are not deep fried. Chinese, Thai, and kebab food outlets all provide choices with lots of 'unrestricted' vegetables along with meat, chicken or seafood. The rice and noodle serving is likely to be large and, if you feel you won't be able to resist the full portion, ask for a half serve.

Supermarkets often have a good selection of frozen and fresh ready-to-go meals. Just check the serving sizes as the same quantity won't be suitable for everyone. Depending on your body makeup you may need to choose the snack-size option and add more 'unrestricted' vegetables. Frozen green vegetables, especially those in steam fresh packets, have improved over the last couple of years. They're a good backup to have in the freezer for either lunch or dinner – just in case!

Great tasting food will allow you to walk away from the table enjoying a delicious sense of contentment.

Stocking the pantry

The following items are handy to have in your pantry or fridge. They all offer quick flavours with very few kilojoules.

Mustards – whole seed, French, mild, hot	Vincotto – delicious drizzled over vegetables or meat and chicken
Worcestershire sauce	Low-kilojoule dressings – the quality has improved in recent years.
Horseradish sauce	
Soy sauce	Jars of salsa – a great low-kilojoule dip or topping for vegetables
Chilli sauce	Jars of crushed garlic
Oyster sauce	Jars of chopped ginger
Hoisin sauce	Capers – provide bursts of Spanish flavour in a salad
Wasabi paste	
Fish sauce	Gherkins
Tomato sauce	Pickled onions
Tomato paste	Artichoke hearts in brine
Beef stock, chicken stock, vegetable stock	Lime juice
Marmite and vegemite	Tinned tomatoes
H P sauce	Tinned asparagus
Mint sauce	Fresh herbs (well worth having a few pots on your windowsill)
Curry paste – red and green	Fresh lemons – for the juice and zest
Balsamic vinegar – the more you spend, the better it is!	Cracked black pepper

12

Happy ever after

Look over your shoulder
Keep routines in place
Use essential supports
Be accountable

Look over your shoulder

The hard work is done when you reach your goal weight, but it's not the end of your journey. The statistics for keeping your weight off do not make good reading. Of those who 'diet' to achieve their weight-loss goal, fewer than 2% will maintain it for more than two years. The reality is that most people will regain their lost weight, along with a little extra, in a reasonably short space of time. But your path of weight loss has been quite different from that for the typical 'dieter'. There's been a strong emphasis on knowing your body makeup and matching it to your food and lifestyle choices. Along the way you've made realistic and sustainable changes. Your understanding of food now goes well beyond the messages on 'healthy' food issued to the public at large. You are aware that you have a history of feeding a bigger person and that you have triggers for eating not always related to hunger. These issues don't just disappear as you lose weight, so you'll need to continue monitoring yourself over the next couple of years.

Along with those who have difficulty in losing weight and keeping it off, there are now people struggling who had no previous weight issues. The global trend with weight is upwards. So you always need to be aware of your 'framework' of food, fluid and exercise – even just to maintain weight. You're doing some very good work for yourself and setting a fine example to your family and those around you. The children of overweight parents have a higher rate of weight gain as they become adults, so

you're not only helping yourself but also helping future generations.

Keep routines in place

You've developed some excellent routines while losing weight, and they should have become part of your daily life. Your 'framework' is a precious tool that has changed your life. With more and more practice it will become your normal pattern. Perhaps you have discovered that old patterns are strong and occasional lapses are predictable. Success is being able to identify when there is a problem, and dealing with it by returning to your 'framework'. Going back to keeping a food diary for a couple of days will put you on track again.

By the time you arrive at your goal weight you may feel very comfortable with your portions. However, over the first year of maintaining weight, your food intake will need to be increased slightly at different stages. Some people do this quite naturally while others will have to make an effort to eat more or their weight will just keep dropping. The initial increase when you arrive at your ideal weight would be an extra one or two portions of either carbohydrate or protein. This could be extra bread at breakfast or lunch, more starchy vegetable at the evening meal, or a larger serving of meat, poultry or fish at one of your meals. It's good to keep the focus on increasing your meals rather than your snacks. A couple of months further on you may notice you are hungrier and

> The hard work is done when you reach your goal weight, but it's not the end of your journey.

again your kilojoule intake will need to be increased, preferably with a focus on the meals. Your weight maintenance will need to be managed for a couple of years. You certainly have more flexibility with your intake at this stage, but monitoring your progress is important. The disappointing statistics for weight maintenance are often a consequence of lack of structure and absence of monitoring, when it's only a matter of time before those old patterns climb back on board!

Use essential supports

While food is the most influential factor involved in weight maintenance, physical activity and good hydration run a close second.

Physical activity during weight loss helps keep you positive and in control with different food choices and portions. While you carry excess body fat, exercise will not be as effective as you would hope in using up kilojoules. But once you have reduced body fat, physical activity – your short brisk daily walks and incidental movement – becomes more important. If you abandon your exercise, it is only a matter of time before other routines fall over, appetite increases, and the weight creeps back on.

Hydration is another strong supporter of appetite control. If you find yourself feeling hungry, check your water intake over the previous couple of days. If the weather was hotter, your alcohol was higher, or you had more salt in a meal (such as with soy sauce), your level of hydration would have been lower if you didn't increase your water accordingly. Sometimes it's surprising how such small factors can make a difference, so take care.

Be accountable

When you've lost your weight, it's likely you'll feel it will never go back on again. Let's hope that's true. But it is wise to put in place as many supports as possible. Weighing yourself every week or two is great for monitoring trends with your weight. However, being accountable to someone other than yourself is also extremely helpful. Often just 2 or 3 visits a year to your dietitian, doctor or practice nurse would be all that is required to check your control. After you have maintained your weight successfully for 2 years, a yearly review would be quite adequate. It's just that little tap on the shoulder in a world that's getting bigger.

13

Recipes – 50 favourites

The more you eat the better
Recipe index

The more you eat the better

Yes, we're talking about your greens! Be as generous as you like with your serves because if you have enough of these 'unrestricted' vegetables on your plate at lunch and dinner, you're less likely to have weight issues. So make them work for you and enjoy the variety of fresh, seasonal tastes. The following '50 favourites' are quick, easy, loaded with flavour – and you can eat as many as you like.

Don't worry about making more than you need. It's great to have a bowl of these vegetables in the fridge for lunch the next day. The sauces and dressings can always be used on your other day-to-day salads and vegetables. Enjoy!

Recipe index

Antipasto Platter

1 pack cherry tomatoes
1 jar artichoke hearts in brine
1 jar red peppers in brine
1 can (184 g) button mushrooms in brine
½ cup balsamic vinegar or
  crema di balsamico

- Put cherry tomatoes in a baking dish and place in a hot oven (200°C) for 5–10 minutes.
- Arrange the remaining ingredients except the vinegar on a large platter.
- Put balsamic vinegar in a small dish and place in the middle.
- Serve with toothpicks and enjoy.
  Makes 6 cups

Asian Coleslaw

500 g green cabbage, finely shredded
1 medium carrot, peeled and grated
1 small onion, peeled and thinly sliced
80 g snowpeas, thinly sliced
½ cup finely chopped fresh coriander

Dressing
3 tbsp lemon or lime juice
1 ½ tbsp freshly grated root ginger
1 clove garlic, peeled and crushed
1 tsp fish sauce
1 tsp chilli sauce
1 tsp brown sugar

- Combine prepared vegetables in a bowl.
- Mix together dressing ingredients and
  toss through vegetables.
  Makes 7–8 cups

Asian Green Beans and Bok Choy

500 g round green beans
1 bunch bok choy
½ cup coarsely chopped fresh
   coriander

Dressing
2 tbsp soy sauce
1 tsp fish sauce
juice of 1 fresh lime
1 tbsp caster sugar
1 tsp finely sliced fresh red chilli

- Trim beans and cut in half.
- Blanch in a saucepan of boiling salted water for 1 minute, then refresh under cold running water.
- Trim white stalk off bok choy and discard. Chop leaves into bite-size pieces. Place in sieve and pour boiling water over to wilt. Refresh under cold water.
- Mix together dressing ingredients and stir well to dissolve sugar.
- Toss dressing through beans, bok choy and coriander.
- Serve hot or cold.

Makes 4 cups

Asparagus and Dill Salad

1 bunch asparagus, about 250 g

Dressing
2 tbsp wholegrain mustard
3 tbsp chopped fresh dill
1 tbsp white balsamic vinegar
zest and juice of ½ lemon
salt and ground black pepper

- Wash asparagus. Snap off woody ends and discard. Cut into diagonal pieces.
- Blanch in a saucepan of boiling salted water for 1 minute, then refresh under cold running water.
- Mix together all dressing ingredients.
- Toss dressing through asparagus.
  Makes 2 cups

Baked Stuffed Red Capsicums

2 red capsicums (peppers)
2 anchovy fillets, chopped and
    soaked in milk
16 capers
½ cup basil leaves
½–1 clove garlic, peeled and
    thinly sliced
½ punnet cherry tomatoes
2 tbsp lite balsamic dressing
whole basil leaves for garnish

- Preheat oven to 180°C.
- Cut capsicums in half lengthways (leave stalks on for a nice presentation), remove seeds and membrane and discard.
- Place capsicums skin-side down into a baking dish,* then fill each shell with:
- ½ an anchovy fillet
- 4 capers
- 3 basil leaves
- 1–2 slivers garlic
- 3–4 cherry tomatoes
- Bake for 30 minutes.
- Sprinkle a small amount of balsamic dressing over each filled shell and garnish with a whole basil leaf.

Makes 2 cups

* Put some crunched-up foil in the bottom of the baking dish to hold capsicums in place.

Beans with Orange and Dill Dressing

400 g round green beans, cut into thirds
salt and ground black pepper

Dressing
2 tbsp orange juice
1 tbsp orange zest
2 tbsp lite honey mustard dressing
2 tsp wholegrain mustard
3 tbsp chopped fresh dill

- Blanch beans in a saucepan of boiling salted water for 1 minute until just tender and still green, then refresh under cold running water.
- Make the dressing by combining ingredients and mixing well.
- Toss dressing through beans and season to taste.
Makes 4 cups

Bok Choy in Oyster Sauce

4 bunches bok choy
½ tsp olive oil
2 spring onions, finely chopped
1 ½ tbsp grated fresh root ginger
3 cloves garlic, peeled and chopped

Sauce
50 ml oyster sauce
1 ½ tbsp low salt soy sauce
1 tbsp Chinese rice wine
1 tsp brown sugar
125 ml chicken stock
2 tsp cornflour

- Trim and wash bok choy under running water.
- Chop bok choy coarsely, then blanch in a saucepan of boiling salted water for 1 minute or until leaves are slightly wilted and stalks are just tender.
- Refresh under cold running water.
- Mix together sauce ingredients.
- Heat a wok or large pan and add oil. Sauté spring onion, ginger and garlic for 10 seconds or until fragrant.
- Add bok choy and stir to heat through.
- Add sauce ingredients to wok and stir until sauce thickens and bok choy is coated.
- Serve immediately.

Makes 4 cups

Braised Red Cabbage

½ tsp olive oil
½ onion, peeled and chopped
1 garlic clove, peeled and crushed
450 g red cabbage, sliced
1 green apple, peeled, cored and diced
2 whole cloves
⅛ tsp freshly grated nutmeg
1 bay leaf
½ cinnamon stick
40 ml red wine
25 ml red wine vinegar
½ tbsp soft brown sugar
250 ml vegetable or chicken stock

- Preheat oven to 150°C.
- Heat oil in a large flameproof casserole dish. Add onion and garlic and cook over medium heat for 5 minutes.
- Add cabbage and cook for a further 10 minutes, stirring frequently.
- Stir through apple, cloves, nutmeg, bay leaf and cinnamon stick.
- Pour in red wine and simmer for 5 minutes.
- Add vinegar, brown sugar and stock.
- Bring to the boil, then cover and cook in the oven for 2 hours.

Makes 7–8 cups

115

Broccoli Salad with Yoghurt Wasabi Dressing

1 head broccoli
1 cup low fat unsweetened plain yoghurt
¼ tsp wasabi paste
½ tsp brown sugar
¼ tsp salt
2 tbsp chopped fresh coriander

- Slice broccoli into florets.
- Blanch broccoli in a saucepan of boiling salted water for 1 minute, then refresh under cold running water. Stalks should be just tender and broccoli itself green.
- Mix together yoghurt, wasabi paste, sugar and salt.
- Toss dressing through broccoli then sprinkle with coriander.
  Makes 2 cups

Broccoli, Tomato and Basil Salad

1 head broccoli
1 punnet cherry tomatoes
2 spring onions
1 bunch basil, coarsely chopped
4 tbsp lite balsamic dressing
salt and ground black pepper

- Cut broccoli into bite-size florets. Blanch in a saucepan of boiling salted water for 1 minute, then refresh under cold running water.
- Cut cherry tomatoes in half, and thinly slice spring onions.
- Combine broccoli, tomatoes, spring onion and basil with dressing and toss to coat.
- Season to taste.
  Makes 4 cups

Broccoli, Cauliflower and Caper Salad

300 g cauliflower florets
200 g broccoli florets
3 spring onions, finely sliced

Sauce
4 tbsp lite honey mustard dressing
2 tbsp low fat unsweetened yoghurt
2 tbsp chopped capers
salt and ground black pepper to taste

- Blanch cauliflower and broccoli florets in a saucepan of boiling salted water for 1 minute, then refresh under cold running water.
- Combine cooked vegetables with spring onions in a large bowl.
- Mix together all sauce ingredients.
- Pour sauce over vegetables and toss well to coat.
  Makes 4 cups

Broccoli with Oyster Sauce

1 head broccoli

Sauce
2 tbsp oyster sauce
2 tbsp low salt soy sauce
2 tbsp sweet chilli sauce
1 cup chopped fresh coriander

- Wash and trim broccoli into florets with long stalks.
- Blanch in a saucepan of salted boiling water for 1–2 munutes until stalks are just tender, then refresh under cold water.
- Mix together sauce ingredients, then toss through warm broccoli.
Makes 2 cups

Brussels Sprouts in Yoghurt Horseradish Dressing

300g Brussels sprouts, trimmed and
  halved
½ cup chopped Italian flat-leaf parsley
  or mint

Dressing
½ cup plain unsweetened yoghurt
4 tsp horseradish sauce
salt and ground pepper to taste

- Place Brussels sprouts in a steamer basket over a saucepan of boiling water. Steam for 2–3 minutes until tender.
- While sprouts are cooking, mix together sauce ingredients.
- Toss the sauce through the sprouts to coat.
- Sprinkle with chopped parsley.
- Serve hot or cold.
  Makes 3 cups

Cabbage with Carrots, Fennel and Lemon

1 medium carrot, peeled
½ tsp olive oil
½ tsp fennel seeds
1 cup finely sliced cabbage
zest and juice of 1 lemon
3 tbsp water
salt and ground black pepper

- Peel carrot into ribbons and set aside.
- Heat oil in a saucepan over moderate heat and add fennel seeds.
- Stir until slightly coloured, then add cabbage, carrot ribbons, lemon zest and water.
- Cover and cook until cabbage has wilted, about 5 minutes.
- Add strained lemon juice and season to taste.

Makes 2 cups

Capsicum and Asparagus in Black Bean Sauce

½ tsp vegetable oil
1 red onion, peeled and cut into wedges
1 red capsicum (pepper), halved,
    deseeded and cut into chunks
1 bunch asparagus, woody ends snapped
    off and cut into 5 cm lengths
2 cloves garlic, peeled and crushed

Sauce
1 tsp cornflour mixed with 3 tbsp water
1 tbsp black bean sauce
2 tbsp sherry

- Heat oil in a wok or large frying pan.
- Add onion, capsicum and asparagus.
- Stir-fry until onion is transparent and asparagus is just tender.
- Add garlic and stir through.
- To make sauce, combine cornflour and water in a small bowl and mix well. Add black bean sauce and sherry.
- Mix sauce into pan to coat vegetables and stir until thickened.
Makes 6 cups

Capsicum with Roast Tomato Relish

1 red capsicum (pepper)
1 punnet cherry tomatoes
salt and ground black pepper
2 cups rocket
1 tbsp light balsamic dressing

- Preheat oven to 200°C.
- Cut capsicum in half, trim and deseed. Place, cut-side down, in a glass or non-stick baking dish and roast for about 15 minutes until slightly charred. Leave oven on.
- Transfer capsicum to a plastic bag and set aside for 10 minutes. Peel off skin and cut capsicum into chunks.
- Wipe out roasting dish and arrange cherry tomatoes in it. Sprinkle with salt and pepper and bake for 15 minutes or until soft and slightly browned.
- Transfer cooked tomatoes to a bowl and roughly mash to make relish.
- Arrange rocket and capsicum chunks on a plate, sprinkle with balsamic dressing and top with tomato relish.

Makes 3 cups

Capsicum Salad

½ tsp olive oil
4 red or yellow capsicums (peppers)
3 whole garlic cloves, skin on
1 large tomato
2 tbsp lite balsamic dressing
1 tbsp Italian flat-leaf parsley

- Preheat oven to 200°C.
- Rub the oil around in a roasting dish.
- Place whole capsicums, garlic cloves and tomato in roasting dish and roast for 15 minutes.
- Remove tomato and garlic from dish and set aside. Turn capsicums over and cook for a further 15 minutes.
- When garlic and tomato are cool enough to handle, peel off skin from both. Cut tomato in half and remove seeds.
- Blend garlic and tomato in a processor with balsamic dressing.
- Transfer capsicums to a plastic bag and set aside for 5 minutes.
- Take capsicums out of plastic bag and remove skin. Slice capsicums and arrange on a platter.
- Cover with dressing and sprinkle with parsley.
Makes 4 cups

Cauliflower and Capsicum with Ginger Sauce

300 g cauliflower florets
½ red capsicum (pepper),
 deseeded and chopped
¼ cup chopped coriander

Sauce
2 tbsp rice vinegar
2 tbsp soy sauce
1 tsp sweet chilli sauce
1 tsp brown sugar
1 tsp finely grated fresh root ginger
1 tsp cornflour
1 tbsp water

- Make sauce first. Combine rice vinegar, soy sauce, chilli sauce, sugar and ginger in a small saucepan and bring to the boil.
- Make a paste with the cornflour and water. Gradually add to sauce in pan and stir as it thickens. Set sauce aside to keep warm.
- Place cauliflower in a steamer basket over a saucepan of boiling water. Steam for 2 minutes until just tender. Steam capsicum pieces in the same way for 30 seconds. Arrange in a serving bowl.
- Sprinkle chopped coriander over vegetables.
- Pour sauce over vegetables and mix well.
- Serve warm.
 Makes 2 cups

Cauliflower Valenciana

250 g cauliflower florets
½ tsp vegetable oil
½ onion, peeled and finely sliced
2 cloves garlic, peeled and crushed
½ x 400 g can chopped tomatoes, drained
100 g flame roasted capsicums (peppers)
   in brine, drained and sliced*
1 tbsp chopped capers
3 tbsp finely chopped fresh basil
½ tsp dried oregano
3–5 drops Tabasco sauce
½ tsp sugar
salt and pepper to taste
2 tbsp chopped Italian flat-leaf parsley

- Blanch cauliflower in a saucepan of boiling salted water for 1 minute or until stems are tender, then refresh under cold running water and set aside.
- In a heavy-bottomed pan heat oil, then gently sauté onion and garlic until soft.
- Stir in tomatoes, capsicum strips, capers, basil, oregano, Tabasco sauce, sugar, and salt and pepper.
- Simmer for 5 minutes, then add cauliflower.
- Stir to heat through, then sprinkle with parsley.

Makes 3 cups

* available in jars from delis and supermarkets

Celery Salad

6 celery stalks, thinly sliced
fresh coriander or parsley sprigs to
   garnish

Dressing
2 tbsp Chinese rice wine
2 tsp soy sauce
1 tbsp soft brown sugar
1 tbsp clear rice vinegar or seasoned
   vinegar for sushi
1 tbsp grated or finely chopped fresh
   root ginger

- Blanch celery in a saucepan of boiling salted water for 1–2 minutes, then refresh under cold running water. Dry thoroughly on a paper towel.
- Arrange celery on a serving dish.
- Combine dressing ingredients and blend well.
- Pour dressing over celery just before serving
- Garnish with coriander or parsley.
Makes 2 cups

Chargrilled Asparagus with Salsa

2 bunches asparagus, woody ends
    snapped off and discarded

Salsa
1 small red onion, peeled and very
    finely chopped
1 red or yellow capsicum (pepper),
    deseeded and diced
2 tbsp chopped fresh basil
2 tbsp lite balsamic dressing

- Cut asparagus stalks in half.
- Mix together salsa ingredients.
- Cook asparagus in a heavy-bottomed
  frying pan or on a barbecue hot plate for
  about 2 minutes, turning at least once,
  until lightly charred.
- Arrange on a platter and top with salsa.
  Makes 2 cups

Chilli Cauliflower

400 g cauliflower (about ½ head),
   cut into small florets
2 tbsp tomato paste
pinch of chilli powder or ¼ fresh red chilli,
deseeded and finely chopped
2 tbsp fresh coriander, chopped
salt and ground black pepper to taste

- Place cauliflower in a steamer basket over a saucepan of boiling water. Steam for 2 minutes until just tender.
- Combine remaining ingredients in bowl and stir through steamed cauliflower to coat.
- Serve hot.
  Makes 4 cups

Chilli Cucumber Salad

1 telegraph cucumber, quartered and deseeded
1 cup roughly chopped or torn fresh coriander leaves

Dressing
2 tsp sweet chilli sauce
2 tbsp rice wine vinegar
1 tsp fish sauce
2 tsp finely chopped fresh root ginger

- Dice cucumber.
- Combine dressing ingredients.
- Toss dressing through cucumber and coriander.
  Makes 2 cups

Choy Sum with Oyster Sauce

1 bunch choy sum
1 tsp finely chopped fresh root ginger
1 clove garlic, peeled and crushed
2 tbsp oyster sauce

- Cut across choy sum to make 4 pieces.
- Heat a little water in the bottom of a wok or frying pan.
- Add ginger and garlic, then choy sum and toss until just wilted.
- Remove from heat, sprinkle with oyster sauce and toss to coat.
- Serve hot.
  Makes 2 cups

Coriander Leeks

1 leek
½ tsp vegetable oil
1–2 cloves garlic, peeled and crushed
1 tbsp dry roasted and crushed
   coriander seeds
2 tbsp white wine
3 tbsp tomato passata*
1 tsp sugar
1 bay leaf
½ tsp dried thyme
1 tsp chilli sauce
salt and ground black pepper
2 tsp lemon zest
2 tsp lemon juice
½ red capsicum (pepper), deseeded and
   finely chopped
¼ cup coarsely chopped fresh coriander

- Slice leek into rounds using mostly the white part and some of the green.
- Heat oil in a frying pan, add garlic and sauté for 2–3 minutes until soft.
- Add crushed coriander seeds, wine, passata, sugar, herbs, chilli sauce, and salt and pepper.
- Bring to a rapid boil, then add the leek and lemon zest.
- Reduce heat down and simmer for 15 minutes until soft.
- Stir through lemon juice, capsicum and fresh coriander.
- Serve hot or cold.

Makes 2 cups

* Buy tomato passata in a jar from the deli or supermarket or make your own by passing canned Italian-style tomatoes through a sieve

Daikon and Cucumber Salad

½ daikon radish, thinly sliced
½ small red onion, peeled and thinly sliced
1 Lebanese cucumber, thinly sliced
30g pink pickled ginger, sliced
1 bunch fresh coriander, chopped
1 bag baby spinach leaves (optional)

Sauce
1 tbsp clear rice wine vinegar
1 tbsp soy sauce

- Combine vegetables in a bowl.
- Pour over the sauce and toss through.
- Spinach can be added to make a more substantial salad.
Makes 3 cups

Eggplant and Mushrooms in Mustard Sauce

½ eggplant (aubergine), halved
    lengthwise then sliced
½ tsp vegetable oil
½ onion, peeled and finely chopped
6 large flat mushrooms, sliced
2 tbsp fresh thyme leaves
salt and pepper to taste

Sauce
¼ cup white wine
1 tbsp chopped capers
1 tsp Dijon mustard
1 tsp wholegrain mustard
juice of ½ lemon
1 tsp cornflour

- Place eggplant in a steamer basket over a saucepan of boiling water. Steam for 1–2 minutes until tender. Set aside.
- Heat oil in a heavy-bottomed saucepan or frying pan and sauté onion for 1 minute on a high heat.
- Add sliced mushrooms and cook for 1 minute.
- Reduce heat to medium and add sauce ingredients to pan and cook for 2 minutes or until sauce has thickened.
- Add sliced eggplant, then gently stir so all vegetables are coated with sauce.
- Sprinkle thyme leaves into pan and season to taste.
- Serve warm.
  Makes 2 cups

Eggplant and Tomato Bake with Gremolata Topping

2 medium eggplants (aubergines),
   trimmed and thinly sliced
1 x 500 g jar tomato pasta sauce
4 tsp fresh thyme leaves

Gremolata topping
1 cup finely chopped parsley
2 cloves garlic, peeled and crushed
zest of 1 lemon

- Preheat oven to 180°C.
- Make a layer of sliced eggplant in an ovenproof dish, spread with ½ cup pasta sauce, then sprinkle with a few thyme leaves.
- Repeat layers until eggplant is finished with a top layer of sauce and thyme leaves.
- Cover with foil and bake for 30–35 minutes until eggplant is tender.
- Meanwhile, combine gremolata ingredients and mix well.
- Remove bake from oven and sprinkle with gremolata topping.
- Serve warm.
  Makes 4 cups

Eggplant Salad with Yoghurt Dressing

2 large tomatoes
¼ tsp salt
½ tsp sugar
1 medium-size eggplant (aubergine)
100 g baby spinach leaves

Dressing
½ cup plain unsweetened low fat yoghurt
½ cup chopped fresh mint
1 tbsp lemon juice
½ tsp sugar
¼ tsp salt
ground black pepper

- Preheat oven to 180°C.
- Core and cut tomatoes into eighths, then arrange wedges on an oven tray and sprinkle with salt and sugar.
- Bake for 30 minutes.
- While tomatoes are baking, slice eggplant into quarters lengthways, then chop into smaller pieces.
- Place eggplant in a steamer basket over a saucepan of boiling water. Steam for 1–2 minutes until tender.
- Arrange cooked tomato and eggplant with spinach leaves in a salad bowl.
- Mix together dressing ingredients and drizzle over salad.
Makes 4 cups

Eggplant with Caper Salsa

1 medium eggplant (aubergine), chopped

Salsa
3 medium tomatoes
100 g capers (reserve a few for garnish)
½ tsp balsamic vinegar
½ tsp brown sugar
sea salt and ground pepper to taste

- Place eggplant in a steamer basket over a saucepan of boiling water. Steam for 1–2 minutes until tender.
- To make salsa, cut tomatoes in half and remove seeds. Blend tomato flesh with remaining salsa ingredients in a food processor until almost smooth.
- Arrange cooked eggplant cubes on a plate and top with salsa.
- Garnish with capers and serve warm or cold.
  Makes 2 cups

Fatoush Salad

¼ red onion, peeled and thinly sliced
½ telegraph cucumber
3 radishes, cut into matchstick-size strips
2 tomatoes, cut into wedges
1 cos lettuce, leaves cut into small pieces
¼ cup chopped fresh mint
2 tbsp lite balsamic vinegar dressing

- Soak onion slices in cold water for 10 minutes.
- Cut cucumber in half lengthwise. Using a spoon remove seeds, then slice thinly.
- Combine onion, cucumber, radish, tomato, lettuce and mint in a salad bowl.
- Toss through dressing and serve immediately.
Makes 4 cups

Ginger Coleslaw

½ red cabbage, shredded
1 carrot, grated
1 tbsp grated fresh root ginger
1 small red onion, peeled and finely sliced
1 cup chopped fresh mint
2 tbsp lite honey and mustard dressing
salt and ground black pepper

- In a large bowl toss all ingredients together with dressing.
- Season to taste.
Makes 6 cups

Greek-style Courgettes

½ tsp olive oil
1 medium onion, peeled and roughly
  chopped
1 tsp coriander seeds
300g courgettes (zucchini), sliced into
  rounds
salt and pepper
¼ cup chopped fresh oregano leaves

Sauce
¼ cup white wine
¼ cup tomato juice
1 tbsp tomato paste
1 tbsp fresh thyme leaves

Mix together in a small bowl

- Heat oil in a heavy-bottomed frying pan.
- Add onion and coriander seeds and gently sauté for 2 minutes.
- Add courgettes then stir in sauce ingredients. Season to taste.
- Cover and cook for 10 minutes at a gentle simmer.
- Stir in chopped oregano leaves.
- Serve warm.
  Makes 4 cups

Green Bean and Dill Salad

250g round green beans, trimmed and
  halved
1 small red onion, peeled and finely sliced
1 bunch fresh dill, finely chopped
salt and ground black pepper

Dressing
1 tbsp white balsamic vinegar
1 tbsp wholegrain mustard
2 tbsp chopped fresh dill leaves

- Blanch beans in a saucepan of boiling
  salted water for 1 minute. Refresh under
  cold running water and drain well.
- Mix together dressing ingredients.
- Place green beans, onion and dill in a
  bowl. Toss through dressing to coat
  vegetables.
- Season to taste.
  Makes 2 cups

Indian Curry Vegetables

150 g cauliflower florets
100 g green beans
100 g courgettes (zucchini), sliced
½ tsp vegetable oil
½ onion, peeled and sliced into thin
    wedges
2 tsp grated fresh root ginger
½ tsp turmeric powder
1 tsp mustard seeds
½ tsp mild curry powder
1 cup chopped canned tomatoes
salt and pepper
½ cup chopped fresh coriander

- Blanch cauliflower, beans and courgettes in a saucepan of boiling salted water for 1–2 minutes, then refresh under cold running water.
- Heat oil in a large frying pan.
- Add onion to pan and gently sauté until soft.
- Stir in ginger, turmeric, mustard seeds and curry powder and stir until fragrant.
- Add tomatoes and heat through, then stir in blanched vegetables along with ½ cup water and allow to heat through.
- Season to taste.
- Serve, sprinkled with coriander.
- **Makes 3 cups**

Italian-style Fennel

1 large or 2 small fennel bulbs
1 courgette (zucchini)
½ tsp vegetable oil
½ small onion, peeled and chopped
1 clove garlic, peeled and crushed
1 tbsp white wine
½ x 400 g can chopped tomatoes
    in juice
2 tbsp chopped capers
1 tsp brown sugar
salt and pepper to taste
¼ cup chopped parsley
2 tbsp chopped fennel fronds

- Trim fennel bulb, then thinly slice lengthwise.
- Cut courgette in half lengthwise, then thinly slice on the diagonal.
- Heat oil in a saucepan or frying pan, then gently sauté onion and garlic until onion is translucent (take care not to burn garlic).
- Add fennel and white wine to pan, and simmer until fennel is just tender.
- Stir in tomatoes, courgettes, capers, brown sugar and salt and pepper.
- Remove from heat and stir through chopped parsley and fennel fronds.
- Serve warm.

Makes 2 cups

Leek and Swede Miso Soup

½ tsp vegetable oil
1 red onion, peeled and finely chopped
150 g swede, peeled and cubed
200 g leeks, washed, trimmed,
   cut lengthwise and finely sliced
3 cups water
1 tsp soy sauce
1 tsp sweet chilli sauce
2 x 20 g sachets miso soup paste

- Heat oil in a saucepan.
- Add onion and sauté until soft.
- Add swede, leeks and water, followed by soy sauce and sweet chilli sauce.
- Simmer for about 5 minutes until swede is tender.
- Just before serving, stir in contents of both miso soup paste sachets and stir to dissolve.
- Serve hot.
  Makes 7–8 cups

Mediterranean Salsa

1 cucumber, cut in half lengthwise and
  seeds removed
3 tomatoes, chopped
1 red or yellow capsicum (pepper),
  deseeded and finely chopped
1 red onion, peeled and finely chopped
1 bunch fresh coriander, chopped
1 tsp sweet chilli sauce
2 tbsp lite balsamic dressing

- Finely chop cucumber. Combine all
  prepared vegetables and coriander in a
  bowl and toss well to mix.
- Add sweet chilli sauce and balsamic
  dressing and toss to coat.
  Makes 6 cups

Minted Green Coleslaw

¼ cabbage
1 stick celery
3 spring onions
½ green capsicum (pepper)
1 cup chopped fresh mint
½ cup chopped fresh parsley
2 tbsp lite honey and mustard dressing
salt and ground black pepper

- Finely slice cabbage, celery and spring onions. Chop and deseed capsicum.
- Toss together all ingredients, add dressing, then season to taste.

Makes 4 cups

Mushroom and Chives with Mustard Dressing

2 cups white button mushrooms
1 tsp wholegrain mustard
2 tbsp lite honey mustard dressing
2 tbsp chopped chives or garlic chives
 salt and pepper

- Wipe mushrooms clean, then finely slice.
- Add mustard to honey mustard dressing and mix well.
- Toss mushrooms and chives in dressing to coat, then season to taste.
  Makes 2 cups

Nam Jhim with a Vegetable Medley

1 cup cauliflower florets
1 cup quartered Brussels sprouts
½ cup green beans, trimmed and sliced
½ cup chopped fresh coriander leaves

Nam Jhim dressing
1 chilli, deseeded and sliced
2 shallots, peeled and chopped
2 roots coriander, washed and
    roughly chopped
1 clove garlic, peeled and
    roughly chopped
1 ½ tbsp brown sugar
¼ cup lime juice
2 tbsp fish sauce

- Cook cauliflower and Brussels sprouts in boiling salted water for 4–5 minutes until just tender.
- Add beans and simmer for 1 minute.
- Drain vegetables, place in a bowl and set aside.
- Pound chilli, shallots, coriander root and garlic in a pestle and mortar or blend in a small food processor.
- Add sugar and pound again. Stir in lime juice and fish sauce and mix well.
- Toss dressing and chopped coriander through just-cooked vegetables.

Makes 3 cups

Oven-roasted Summer Salad

1 red onion, peeled and chopped into chunky pieces
2 red capsicums (peppers), deseeded and thickly sliced
4 courgettes (zucchini), trimmed and cut into batons
5 tomatoes, quartered
1 punnet cherry tomatoes
½ cup fresh thyme leaves (reserve some for garnish)
3 tbsp balsamic vinegar
3 tbsp lite balsamic dressing
sea salt and ground black pepper

- Place a sheet of baking paper in bottom of roasting dish. Add prepared onion and capsicum.
- Bake for 15–20 minutes until onion is soft.
- Add courgette, quartered tomatoes and cherry tomatoes. Sprinkle with thyme leaves, then drizzle with the balsamic vinegar.
- Bake for another 20 minutes or until vegetables are soft.
- Remove from oven and set aside to cool.
- Place cooled vegetables into a serving dish. Sprinkle with balsamic dressing, sea salt, pepper and garnish with reserved fresh thyme leaves.

Makes 4 cups

Ratatouille

1 tsp olive oil
1 onion, peeled and chopped
2 cloves garlic, peeled and crushed
½ eggplant (aubergine), cut into chunks
½ each green, yellow and red capsicum
    (pepper), deseeded and cut into chunks
1 courgette (zucchini), halved lengthwise,
then sliced
125 g white mushrooms, quartered
½ x 400 g can chopped tomatoes or
    cherry tomatoes
½ tsp brown sugar
¼ tsp dried thyme
¼ tsp dried basil
¼ tsp salt
pepper to taste
¼ cup chopped fresh basil
¼ cup chopped fresh marjoram
¼ cup chopped fresh parsley

- Heat oil in a saucepan. Add onion and garlic and sauté for 3–4 minutes until soft.
- Add eggplant and capsicum to pan and cook for 10 minutes, stirring occasionally.
- Add courgette, mushroom, tomatoes, brown sugar, dried herbs and seasoning.
- Reduce heat and cook, covered, for 20 minutes, stirring occasionally.
- Remove lid and cook for a further 15 minutes.
- Stir through fresh herbs and serve hot or at room temperature.

Makes 6 cups

Red Cabbage, Orange and Mint Salad

2 cups sugar snap peas
½ small red cabbage, finely shredded
2 oranges, peeled and segmented
1 tbsp chopped fresh mint
1 tbsp orange juice
2 tbsp lite balsamic dressing

- Blanch sugar snap peas in a saucepan of boiling salted water for 1 minute, then refresh under cold running water.
- Combine blanched peas, cabbage, orange segments and mint in a bowl and mix well.
- Toss with orange juice and dressing
  Makes 4 cups

Red Summer Salad

3 red capsicums (peppers), halved and
   deseeded
4 medium tomatoes, sliced
½ red onion, peeled and finely chopped
½ cup shredded fresh basil leaves
3 tbsp lite balsamic dressing
salt and ground black pepper

- Preheat oven to 180°C.
- Place capsicums, cut-side down, on an oven tray and bake until skin starts to blacken.
- Transfer capsicums to a plastic bag and set aside for 10 minutes. Remove skin from capsicum and discard. Slice capsicum.
- Combine everything in a bowl and sprinkle with dressing.
- Season to taste.
  Makes 6 cups

Roasted Red Capsicums with Capers and Thyme

6 red capsicums (peppers), halved and
   deseeded
2 tbsp chopped capers
2 tbsp chopped thyme leaves
2 tbsp light balsamic dressing

- Preheat oven to 180°C.
- Place capsicums, cut-side down, in an ovenproof dish and roast for approximately 10 minutes or until slightly charred.
- Transfer capsicums to a plastic bag and set aside for 10 minutes. Remove skin from capsicum and discard. Cut roasted capsicum halves into chunks.
- Mix together capers, thyme and dressing.
- Toss dressing through capsicum chunks to coat.
  Makes 2 cups

Sautéed Artichokes, Beans and Rosemary

200 g round green beans,
   diagonally sliced
½ tsp olive oil
2 spring onions, diagonally sliced
3 sprigs rosemary, stalks discarded
1 tbsp capers
1 x 400 g can artichoke hearts in brine,
   drained and cut into quarters
2 tbsp lite balsamic dressing
salt and ground black pepper

- Blanch sliced beans in boiling salted water for 1 minute, then refresh under cold running water. Drain well.
- Heat oil in a large frying pan.
- Add beans, spring onion and rosemary leaves.
- Cook for 1–2 minutes or until lightly browned.
- Stir in capers and artichokes to heat through.
- Transfer vegetables to a bowl and toss with balsamic dressing.
- Season to taste and serve warm or cold.
Makes 4 cups

Summer Vegetable Salad with Chinese Dressing

100 g snowpeas, trimmed and
    sliced diagonally
150 g courgettes (zucchini), halved
    lengthwise and sliced diagonally
100 g button mushrooms, thinly sliced
1 red capsicum (pepper), deseeded and
    thinly sliced
½ cup chopped Italian flat-leaf parsley

Chinese dressing
1 tsp grated fresh root ginger
1 clove garlic, peeled and crushed
2 tbsp rice wine vinegar
1 tbsp soy sauce

- Blanch snow peas for 1 minute in boiling salted water, then refresh under cold running water and set aside.
- Toss prepared vegetables in a large bowl with dressing.
- Allow to stand for 15 minutes to absorb dressing and develop flavours.
- Just before serving, sprinkle with parsley and toss gently.

Makes 4 cups

Sweet and Sour Vegetables

½ tsp vegetable oil
1 medium red onion, peeled and chopped
2 cloves garlic, peeled and crushed
1 tsp finely chopped fresh root ginger
150 g cauliflower florets
¼ cup water
100 g green round beans, trimmed and
  chopped
1 courgette (zucchini), halved lengthwise,
  then chopped
1 red capsicum (pepper), deseeded and
  chopped
1 handful fresh coriander, chopped

Sauce
¼ cup sweet and sour sauce (available
  from supermarkets)
1 tsp sweet chilli sauce
2 tsp soy sauce

Mix together and set aside

- Heat oil in a heavy-bottomed saucepan or
  frying pan.
- Add onion, garlic and ginger to pan and
  sweat for 1 minute.
- Add cauliflower and water. Cover and gently
  cook until cauliflower is almost tender.
- Stir in beans and cook for 1 minute further
  until just tender, but still bright green.
- Mix together ingredients for sauce and add
  to pan with courgette and capsicum.
- Stir, then gently simmer for 1–2 minutes or
  until vegetables are heated through.
- Remove from heat and toss with coriander.
- Serve warm.
  Makes 7–8 cups

Water Chestnuts and Capsicum in Plum Sauce

½ tsp vegetable oil
1 medium onion, peeled and chopped
1 tsp grated fresh root ginger
2 cloves garlic, peeled and crushed
1 yellow capsicum (pepper), deseeded and chopped
1 x 250 g can whole water chestnuts, drained
1 tbsp sweet plum sauce
1 tbsp oyster sauce
½ cup chopped Italian flat-leaf parsley

- Heat oil in a saucepan or frying pan.
- Add onion and sauté for 4–5 minutes until transparent.
- Stir in ginger and garlic, then capsicum. Sauté for 1 minute (add a little water if too dry).
- Add water chestnuts, plum sauce and oyster sauce and stir to heat through.
- Remove from heat and add parsley.
- Serve warm.
  Makes 2 cups

About the author

MaryRose Spence BHSc NZ Registered Dietitian

MaryRose graduated from Otago University with a degree in nutrition. She completed a postgraduate year at Wellington Hospital to become a New Zealand registered dietitian.

She spent the following ten years overseas working as a dietitian in Australia, England and Saudi Arabia. The great diversity of cultures she has worked with and their varied associated difficulties have enabled MaryRose to develop a wider than usual knowledge base. Her experiences have enabled her to be particularly resourceful in terms of helping with specific client needs.

MaryRose returned to Auckland twenty years ago and established The Nutrition Consultants – a busy private dietetic practice that provides advice on a wide range of nutritional issues. During this time MaryRose saw first hand the difficulties and poor results that dieting offers and in her campaign to provide an easier, more successful and more permanent way to weight loss she developed the WeightWise programme.

Her book *Size Does Matter* is based on this programme.

MaryRose is a well-known and highly regarded authority on weight loss and nutrition. Working closely with GPs and the wider medical profession, she is a regular presenter of nutritional advice at many levels in the community, and is frequently consulted for her expert opinion on both radio and television. She featured most recently as an authority on the television series *What's Really in our Food?*

With training from the Cordon Bleu School in London and an active membership in The Food Writers Guild of New Zealand, MaryRose has built a reputation for offering a blend of straightforward, effective guidelines for food and lifestyle with trustworthy, up-to-the-minute nutritional information.

MaryRose is happily married with two teenage children.

For more information on the WeightWise programme visit www.weightwise.co.nz.

First published in 2011 by WeightWise Ltd,
580 Remuera Road, Auckland 1050, New Zealand
www.weightwise.co.nz

1 3 5 7 9 10 8 6 4 2

ISBN: 978-0-473-19091-0

A catalogue record for this book is available from the
National Library of New Zealand

Design: Trevor Newman
Photography: John Daley Photography Ltd

Printed in China through Bookbuilders.